I'm Almost Out of Cha:
Woody Paige's Chalkboard Tales

by

Woody Paige

Foreword by
Tony Reali

Vigliano Books

This book is a work of fiction. Names, characters, places and incidents are either the product of the author's imagination or are used fictitiously. Any resemblance to actual persons, living or dead, or to actual events or locales is entirely coincidental.

Cover design by Vigliano Books

Interior and cover images by Jason Weindruch

Published by Vigliano Books
http://www.viglianoassociates.com

Digital design by Telemachus Press, LLC
http://www.telemachuspress.com

Visit the author website:
http://www.woodypaige.com

ISBN# 978-1-940745-29-9 (paperback)

Version 2014.01.21

Printed in the United States of America

10 9 8 7 6 5 4 3 2 1

Dedicated to Shannon Hunt Paige.

I always call her my favorite daughter. She is my only daughter. She is the best daughter in the world. I offered my only piece of advice when she was a young girl, and it has become our favorite family quote. One recent Christmas she gave me a photo from the James Bond movie *Goldfinger*. In it, Goldfinger is standing aside a laser. Bond is strapped to a table, and the red laser beam is ascending between his legs toward his crotch. "Do you expect me to talk, Goldfinger," Bond says anxiously. "No, Mr. Bond, I expect you to die."

On the photo my daughter printed the word
"PERSERVERANCE", followed by our quote:

"Don't let the bastards get you down."

Shannon and I don't. Take our advice: Neither should you.

"If you can't annoy somebody, there is little point in writing."
—Kingsley Amis in "Lucky Jim"

"I hate quotations. Tell me what you know."
—Ralph Waldo Emerson

"If two people always agree, one of them is unnecessary."
—Henry Ford

Table of Contents

I'm Almost Out of Cha:

Woody Paige's Chalkboard Tales

Foreword

For as long as I've known Woodrow Wilson Paige, Jr. (up to the minute that's 10 years, 2,040 shows, 454 Face Times and 16,365 mutes!!!) he's been a man of words. It would be somewhat awkward for *The Denver Post* and *Around the Horn* if he weren't. But Woody's words are not like yours or mine. They are unique; at one moment face palms of wisdom, at another riddles wrapped in mysteries inside enigmas finished by Mad Libs trying to find Where's Waldo. How he does it I'll never know. I mean, I'm the one who has to try to score his argument every day and most the time I can't see the forest through the trees. Or so I'm told.

Woody's words have been around the world more than they've been *Around the Horn*. He's covered over 10,000 sporting events. (Think about that for a second. *10,000 sporting events.* Take your 10,000 measly hours and stick it, Malcolm Gladwell). In one unforgettable, heart wrenching column Woody used his words to talk about his own battle with depression. I was in New York the night the American Foundation for Suicide Prevention honored him with a Public Education Award for that column. When Woody used his words to accept that award there wasn't a dry eye in Lincoln

Center. A man of great many words. A man of great words. A great man of words.

But how did we get here, a book about words written in chalk … in the background of a shot taken by a robocam … near the Obituaries Department in the office of *The Denver Post?* Only Woody can answer that but I'll say this; if there's one thing that years of meeting people at games/restaurants/Medieval Times has told me it's that the two most likeable personalities on *Horn* (and possibly *ESPN)* are a blackboard and a mute button. One giveth and the other taketh away. And while the mute is in the hands of a fickle haircut, the blackboard belongs to all. By the people, for the people. So it's not just Woody's inner voice, it's the people's voice. And it's a voice that needs to be heard. In this mysterious world we Horn in, words are at a premium (I sometimes ask the panel, "One syllable or less, Yes or No?" Woody invariably answers, "OK."). Mute and elimination wait around every corner. An immutable shadow is a most valuable commodity.

When Woody first hung Chalkie up in 2004 I thought he would run out of material by the second commercial break. In the 10 seasons since there's been over *7,000!* From the sublime *(This is my brain. This is my brain on chalk)* to the subliminal *(TELAM PLAYER)* to the subconscious *(I keep hitting the 'escape' button on my laptop but I don't)*, he's more dependable than Depends. How he's continued to come up with them is a secret I hope he divulges in the pages ahead. I honestly don't know. I tell people he must be using PECs; Phrase Enhancing Chalk. They're Woody-isms. And what started as Woody-isms around the newsroom became the blackboards on the show that turned into the book you're reading now which saves you the trouble of lugging 7,000 chalkboards into the bathroom.

One thing that needs to be said that's somewhat easy to overlook; all this predates Facebook and Twitter. 2004 was a simpler time, children. If someone wanted people to know that "LOL—these mozz cheez stix r da bomb:)" or "Second colonoscopy this week!! #swag #twerk #ridindirty #colonolol" they'd actually have to leave their house and speak the words to another human. It was a pastime called talking; ask Wikipedia about it. My point is, in this near prehistoric time the only place you could get status updates, jokes and puns of puns in a user friendly 140 character clip (while still triumphantly minimizing human interaction!!!) was Woody's chalkboard. Voilà, the first Facebook and Twitter. It makes you wonder how Woody's not making gazillions off this. Or, *more* gazillions if you're reading this in the hardcover form.

Speaking of gazillion dollar business ideas, here's to the next edition of this chalkboard book about chalkboards actually *being a chalkboard!*

All of the quotes you'll find in this book appeared on *Around the Horn* at some point in the first ten years of the program. But there's one I can guarantee (**note from Woody: no guarantees are guaranteed**) you won't be seeing: May 19, 2010. It read:

ADVERTISE
HERE:
1-800
555-HORN

It might have sent dozens (hundreds? millions?!?) to *"the hottest phone answering service around."* Oops. See, it appears the letters H-O-R-N coincidentally, I repeat **_coincidentally_**, share the same digits as a, how do you say, telephonic sexy-time provider. If you happened to call that number (EARMUFFS!) a sultry voice that sounded like it just smoked the exhaust pipe off a Hyundai greeted you with the numbers to press to reach a very attentive associate of hers, whilst putting a curious emphasis on your need to push the POUND button. I can't imagine what all those off-duty nurses/babysitters/French maids/female prison guards were thinking when the calls started to flood in at 5:03 pm Eastern. Needless to say Chalkie had to go on "vacation" for a few days.

Now you might think that between that "vacation" and the roaming rates that our background hero would be compelled into an early retirement, forced to spend its last days as all good chalkboards do; tic-tac-toe at Del Boca Vista. You might think that. Take a look at Woody's message on Chalkie's first show back:

SCARY THOUGHT:
I'M THE SMART
ONE ON
THIS PANEL

Only The Drow.

If we were on *Around the Horn* and a panelist tried to end their FaceTime with a quote it would be the mating call of the mute button (unless it was a quote from *Goodfellas*.) But since this entire book is quotes I'll play along and dust off an old one. English essayist Samuel Johnson, (0 career wins, 0 career mutes) in between some really long poems and an entire critique of the English language, (True story. Also true: when I googled "Samuel Johnson" auto-type directed me to Samuel L. Jackson) once said "Life itself is a quotation." That brings us to Woody's chalkboard on October 4, 2013:

"LIFE"

That's life. And that's Woody Paige, ladies and gentlemen. Now let's start living one chalkboard at a time.

~Tony Reali, October 14, 2013

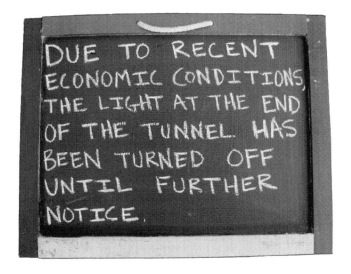

Troglodytes should be credited with creating the original chalkboard quote.

Some prehistoric smart-ass probably scribbled on a cave wall, "This is so easy even a sports writer could do it."

And: "It's later than we think."

He was right.

But, then, the Cro-Magnon was so dumb he stared at the orange juice carton for 30 minutes after seeing the word 'Concentrate.' Rimshot.

*   *   *   *

Four of us were returning from dinner in the Chelsea area of New York City when a man approached, introduced himself as "Maurice," announced he was homeless and asked me for a donation. I handed him a dollar.

"You my man," he exclaimed. "I love the sayings on the chalkboard."

"But you said you're homeless," I replied. "You can't have a TV. How would you know?"

"Cause I watched you on TV the past 10 years in prison."

*   *   *   *

Just before I finished this book, I sat in an Indianapolis hotel bar on a Saturday night, watching college football on ESPN.

A guy walked into the bar (which is how most jokes starts, but this is a true story), looked at the empty stool and said, "Mind if I sit here?"

"No, but you wouldn't have been my first choice."

The bartender said to the guy, "Don't mind him. He's a professional smart-ass (troglodyte)."

"Oh, how does one become a professional smart-ass? What do you do?"

I pointed to the TV and said: "I work for them."

He said: "You work for LG?"

LG is the company that built the flat-screen TV.

"Sure," and I went back to writing possible chalkboard quotes on a bar napkin. *I like getting old; it beats the alternative.*

*　　*　　*　　*

As I finished interviewing Bob Costas for a magazine story, I asked what he would like his legacy to be. After he answered very eloquently and seriously, Bob added,

"I know what your legacy will be; the blackboard quotes."

I sighed. "You're a world-famous broadcaster. You've hosted the Olympics and been involved in every other major sports event on the globe, from the World Series to the Kentucky Derby. You'll be honored with a memorial in some cemetery or ballpark. And when I'm buried, I won't even have a tombstone. There'll be a chalkboard above my grave with the quote, 'I told you I was sick. My mind, too.'"

Just like the homeless man, Bob said, "I love the blackboard quotes."

Then he asked the question I've gotten thousands of times over the past eight years: *"Where do you come up with them?"*

"A lot I write on cocktail napkins," I said.

"Well … that is something you would know about."

Thanks Bob, for insinuating, correctly, that I'm a barfly. Bob first interviewed me during halftime at an American Basketball Association game in 1973. He was the young hotshot radio play-by-play man on KMOX for the Spirits of St. Louis, and I was the

Memphis Tams' beat writer for The Commercial Appeal news-paper. Surely, you remember those two extinct pro-basketball teams? Since then, Bob and I have covered every sport imaginable. He is known for being the best and most knowledgeable on NBC. I'm known for playing a goof on cable sports news. We've come quite a ways from that night in St. Louis.

Bob has written best-selling books about baseball. I'm writing a book about chalkboard quotes.

*   *   *   *

When the chalkboard first hit the air, I didn't know if the audience would get it. Not the jokes, you'd have to be Cro-Magnon not to get them, but I half-expected viewers to point at me in the street and say, 'There's the idiot who needs a chalkboard to tell him what to do.'

I covered a college football game in Boulder, Colorado. At halftime I wandered over to look at a new addition to the stadium (I have no life) and a bunch of college students kept coming up to me and saying how they watched *the show* daily and loved the banter and the fun, and that there was a national Woody Paige drinking game on college campuses. Every time I was muted (a gimmick on the show to punish panelists whose answers host Max Kellerman didn't agree with) students everywhere would do a shot of tequila or vodka. "Stop getting muted so much. We're drunk 10 minutes into the show!" one young man laughed.

A young lady walked over, pointed at me and screamed "You're Bobby Paige!"

"No, I'm not," I protested.

"Yes, you are," she said. "My boyfriend and I watch you every day. He's your biggest fan."

"But I'm not Bobby Paige. I'm …"

But she wouldn't stop. "Yesterday, when the show was on, we were making love (only she didn't say making love), and he was watching you and saying how funny you were. Would you sign an autograph for him?"

"Sure. What's his name?" She said Tom. I wrote, '*Tom: Thanks for being a faithful viewer. Every day while I'm doing the show I'll think about you doing your girlfriend.*'

And I signed it, '*Love, Bobby Paige.*'

The young lady said: "See, I told you you're Bobby Paige."

*   *   *   *

That night I slept peacefully and soundly for the first time in quite a while. I said to myself, 'Self, who did you think you were Walter Freaking Cronkite?!' I'm just a sports columnist who patterned his TV personality after Soupy Sales and Dan Reeves. Most of you don't even know who Soupy Sales was. He hosted an afternoon TV show for kids when I was a kid. It actually was for adults. And I thought it was the greatest TV show. Never missed it. He once told all the boys and girls that they should sneak into their parents' bedroom, get all the green paper they could find in their wallets and purses, and send it to Soupy. Sure enough, a whole bunch of youngsters did. And when Soupy got thousands of dollars in the mail, he got into legal trouble.

I know what that's like.

I've buried the lead, as I've been told a few times in 50 years of journalism.

Thousands of viewers, literally, have asked over the years when I intended to write a book reprinting all the chalkboard sayings.

Well, here it is, finally.

Not all of them, though. There are about 2,000 chalkboard quotes (out of more than 7,500 over the years) in these pages. Some are good, bad, ugly, awful, indifferent and interesting. Coming up with three chalkboard quotes a day, 3-5 days a week, about 200 times a year, is not so easy a Neanderthal can do it. It's HARD.

Let's start with 25 of my favorites (in no particular order):

I'm confused. Oh, wait, maybe I'm not

*   *   *   *

I was not informed that the bird is the word

*   *   *   *

My life has been influenced more by
Play-Doh than Plato

*   *   *   *

I just finished a two-week diet;
all I lost was 14 days

*   *   *   *

Ten reasons to procrastinate: No 1.
(I'll tell you all of them later)

*   *   *   *

Errors have been made. Others will be blamed

*   *   *   *

My hamster died yesterday
Fell asleep at the wheel

* * * *

Bill Plaschke, you're not yourself today
I noticed the improvement immediately

* * * *

If you don't think anybody is paying attention to
you, just miss making a payment

* * * *

The people on Around The Horn who know the
least argue the most

* * * *

Do I look like a people person?

* * * *

If you don't pay your exorcist,
you'll get repossessed

* * * *

I keep hitting the 'escape' button on my laptop,
but I don't

* * * *

Sometimes I wake up Grumpy … Sometimes I
just let her keep on sleeping

* * * *

Save the Earth; it's the only planet with chocolate

* * * *

I don't bring anything to the table but my appetite

* * * *

You better back up;
I don't know how loud I'm going to get

* * * *

Our holiday fruitcakes have no expiration date

* * * *

So far, this is the oldest I've ever been

* * * *

I've always looked up to my elders,
but now, at my age, I have none

* * * *

Dear Algebra: Stop trying to get us to find your
X … She's not coming back

* * * *

This is my brain. Well, this is my brain on chalk

* * * *

Love is grand; divorce is five hundred grand

* * * *

Keep on talking;
I always have this bored look on my face

* * * *

Buckle up!
I'm about to show you some geography

* * * *

I didn't say they were 25 of the best. Those are ahead, I hope.
You'll decide.

As so many others have done, please send me some of your ideas for the chalkboard to woody@woodypaige.com. I'll pick out a few and send the winners personalized chalkboards.

I'm about to take you for an e-ticket Mr. Frog's Wild Ride through the chalkboard quote jungle. To Maurice, Bob Costas, Tony Reali, the drinking game players at various colleges, the guy at the bar, the cavemen and all the rest of you:

Enjoy!

2

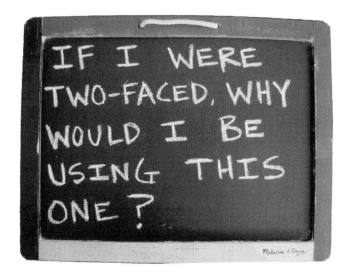

I've covered more than 40 Super Bowls, along with 32 Masters golf tournaments, about two dozen World Series, 14 Summer and Winter Olympics, a couple of Stanley Cup Finals, 15 NBA Finals, every major college football bowl (including the Orange, the Rose, the Fiesta, the Cotton, the Sugar, the Liberty, the Gator, the New Mexico, the Holiday and the Weedeater bowls), the BCS Championship seven or eight times, the Final Four 20 times, the Kentucky Derby, the Indianapolis 500 six straight years, NASCAR and Grand Prix races, several U.S. Opens in tennis and golf, Wimbledon and the British Open a bunch of times (you forget numbers after a while) and every other major event you can think of. Championship boxing bouts in Vegas (from Muhammad Ali to Mike Tyson), the very first pay-per-view Ultimate Fighting Championship, pro bowling tournaments, professional wrestling, the World Cup in soccer twice, NFL games in London, Tokyo, Berlin and Mexico City, a major league baseball opener in Mexico, NBA games in every league city, all-star games in the major sports (including soccer), world skiing championships, track (and sometimes field) championships, spring training for 30 seasons in Arizona and Florida, and I think it adds up to, over 50 years, close to 10,000 games.

One week in Sydney, Australia, I watched soccer, rugby, Aussie Rules football and NFL football. One Olympics Monday in Los Angeles in 1984 (yes, Orwell's 1984) I attended 20 different sports competitions. I saw The Dream Team in Barcelona and was with the players when they held training—ha!—in Monte Carlo (and played Blackjack with Michael Jordan and Charles Barkley). I saw Tiger Woods win his first major (the Masters), the U.S. Open at Torrey Pines and his British Opens at St. Andrews. I stood on the bank of a river in Ireland and talked to Tiger as he fished, and I stood on a hill and talked to him after his last major victory. I saw Jordan win four of his NBA titles and John Elway lose three Super Bowls and win two.

So I've been around the block (and driven around the oval at Indy and flown with the U.S. Navy's Blue Angels).

*   *   *   *

The chalkboard is like a faithful dog, my constant companion. Chalkboards; I've had about four dozen over the years, and currently own six. I buy them (they are more expensive than you might think) from a small husband-and-wife company called Melissa & Doug. I have traveled with a blackboard everywhere from Detroit to New York, Miami Beach (we actually did the show from the beach) to Old Scottsdale (I gave the blackboard to a wounded warrior in a wheelchair, and it has a better home now), the Florida Keys, Atlanta, Washington D.C. (we went to the Washington Monument together), Boston (and nearby Walden Pond), San Diego (where we went to a bar, and a woman picked up, literally, the blackboard, not me), Los Angeles and parts unknown.

I never check the chalkboard with my luggage. You never know when somebody will want to steal a chalkboard.

At the airport in Tampa , after I went through security, I was pulled aside by a TSA agent. "Will you come with me, sir?" I don't own a gun or do illegal drugs (although marijuana, as you may have heard, is sold legally in Colorado, but, when I tried the weed in college, it either made me sleepy, or see snakes, or want to eat six Whoppers at one sitting, so that was enough). I do try to sneak mouthwash through security. ("What are you in prison for?" "Mouthwash.")

I was taken into a nearby room where six security officers were standing. What? One was holding the blackboard. It had been apprehended. "We all love the sayings on the blackboard. Would you mind taking a photo with us and the blackboard and writing on it 'TSA security rocks?'"

"Sure. But I'm going to miss my flight."

"We'll drive you to the gate in a cart."

"Will you turn on the siren?"

*   *   *   *

Here are 99 more chalkboard quotes:

I'm up and out of bed. What more do you want?

*   *   *   *

I'd rather be fighting zombies

*   *   *   *

Don't interrupt the conversation
I'm having with myself

*   *   *   *

I'm gonna invent a vaccine for stupid

*   *   *   *

Can we have class outside today?

*   *   *   *

If you don't like my driving, stay off the sidewalk

*   *   *   *

Sorry for being myself

*   *   *   *

Sorry for shouting yesterday

*   *   *   *

Sorry for being so loud last segment

*   *   *   *

I'm just a sorry person

*   *   *   *

The glass is always full: half air, half water

*   *   *   *

Restraint is good in moderation

*   *   *   *

Snowmen fall from the sky unassembled

*   *   *   *

Sure, let me drop everything
and work on your problem!

*   *   *   *

Pain is weakness leaving the body

*   *   *   *

Hi! I don't care. Thanks! Have a nice day

*   *   *   *

Each show with Tony Reali
makes me appreciate my dog more

*   *   *   *

Stop here on mute

*   *   *   *

Whew! I just finished returning
all my Christmas gifts

*   *   *   *

No more gift cards. Just send cash!

*   *   *   *

Vegas says I have a 1% chance to win today

*   *   *   *

I never liked a man I didn't meet

*   *   *   *

I can walk the walk and chalk the chalk

*   *   *   *

Duct tape fixes everything _ and is the only thing
other than a mute button that can shut me up!

*   *   *   *

I'm excited for a new year;
I have another chance to get it right

*   *   *   *

May all your troubles last as long as your
New Year's resolutions!

*   *   *   *

Christmas isn't just a day; it's a frame of mind

*   *   *   *

Well, it's cold outside. A man's gotta do
something to keep warm

*   *   *   *

You better watch out, you better not cry, Tim
Tebow is coming to town

*   *   *   *

Now Dasher, now Dancer, now Prancer, now
Vixen, on Comet, on Cupid, on Donder, on Reali

*   *   *   *

You know you're getting old,
when Santa looks younger than you

*   *   *   *

Let's be naughty and save Santa the trip

*   *   *   *

I saw mommy kissing Santa Claus,
and so did daddy

*   *   *   *

A Christmas shopper's complaint is
one of long standing

*   *   *   *

Ship your gifts today,
so they can be lost by Christmas

*   *   *   *

Santa has the right idea:
Visit people only once a year

*   *   *   *

Here today, gone to borrow

*   *   *   *

Support the right to arm bears

*   *   *   *

So hip it hurts

*   *   *   *

If you want something that'll last forever,
take out a mortgage!

*   *   *   *

How can a person draw a blank?

*   *   *   *

I want a ginger bread condo

*   *   *   *

Chocolate covered cherries are the pits

*   *   *   *

Why can't chestnuts be roasted on a closed fire?

*   *   *   *

We do not accept returns,
but we reject yours with a smile

*   *   *   *

I reject your reality and substitute my imagination

*   *   *   *

All exchanges must be made within 6 minutes

*   *   *   *

Yesterday was the deadline for all complaints

*   *   *   *

I barely survived yesterday. And it's today already!

*   *   *   *

After Kevin Blackistone talks there's still
meat left on that bone

*   *   *   *

Efficiency is intelligent laziness

*   *   *   *

A man is known by the company he avoids

*   *   *   *

The early bird gets the worm.
The early dog gets the bird

*   *   *   *

Won an Emmy last night for Best Facetime

*   *   *   *

Warning: mouth operates faster than brain

*   *   *   *

It's my time to shine!

*   *   *   *

When fish are in schools,
they sometimes take debate

*   *   *   *

Those who get too big for their britches
will be exposed in the end

* * * *

Medicine is the best medicine

* * * *

Now that I know all the answers,
nobody ask me any questions

* * * *

An unemployed court jester is nobody's fool

* * * *

Why are they called "stands" when
they're made for sitting?

* * * *

Everything can be filed under "miscellaneous"

* * * *

Act now: I'm available for 4 difficult payments of
$19.99

* * * *

Someone claimed I sound like an owl. Who?

* * * *

I went from liking Air Supply to
needing air supply

* * * *

Salt and pepper to taste

* * * *

Either you agree with me, or you're wrong

* * * *

Forgive Bomani Jones; I was young and
stupid once, too

*   *   *   *

I'd rather be alone than with these people

*   *   *   *

I'm your wing, man

*   *   *   *

Pong is still the best video game

*   *   *   *

I've got your front;
you have to take care of your own back

*   *   *   *

The only thing we have to fear is fear itself …
and mutes!

*   *   *   *

Cool story bro; tell it again,
only slower and better this time

*   *   *   *

The triangle said to the circle: You're pointless

*   *   *   *

Bob Ryan and I are reprising our roles as the two
old men on *The Muppets* show

*   *   *   *

All sports are fantasy sports with this body

*   *   *   *

I'm just the boy that tweeted "wolf"

*   *   *   *

Karaoke is a window to the soul
Soul, or funk, or rock

*   *   *   *

Give me Facetime, or give me cheeseburgers

*   *   *   *

Beggars can't be choosers,
but they can win this show!

*   *   *   *

If you don't believe me, I made it up

*   *   *   *

I like Vanna White better than Tony Reali

*   *   *   *

All true wisdom is found on this board

*   *   *   *

Never eat a powdered donut
when wearing a dark suit

*   *   *   *

Never stand between a dog and a fire hydrant

*   *   *   *

You must be this tall to be an ATH champ

*   *   *   *

Pithy comment goes here

*   *   *   *

Chickens playing basketball ... flagrant fowl

*   *   *   *

If Rome were built in a day,
I would hire that contractor

*   *   *   *

Tony should give me a point for punctuation.!?

*   *   *   *

I am even more handsome if
you watch me on podcast

*   *   *   *

It wasn't a lie;
it was ineptitude with insufficient cover

*   *   *   *

The only thing worse than not getting what you
want, is someone else getting it

*   *   *   *

If you don't like what's being said,
change the conversation

*   *   *   *

I can't believe *Dancing With the Stars*
isn't returning my phone calls

*   *   *   *

Why does the "election season" last for 3 seasons?

*   *   *   *

Honk if you love the chalkboard

*   *   *   *

My chalkboard is smarter than your honor student

*   *   *   *

Don't talk to me, I'm arguing

*   *   *   *

I'm not saying you're paranoid,
but everyone knows you are

*   *   *   *

Hug your local chalkboard

*   *   *   *

This board is also an accurate topographical map
of North Dakota

*   *   *   *

My NCAA basketball bracket is in worse shape
than my abs

*   *   *   *

Gravy is an underrated condiment

*   *   *   *

Warning: I do stupid things!

*   *   *   *

I'm a ninja on weekends

*   *   *   *

Teiam player

*   *   *   *

F n h th s nt ce

*   *   *   *

When you're board with your budget,
you run out of chalk

*   *   *   *

My imaginary friend thinks
Tony Reali has serious problems

*　　*　　*　　*

Shut your mouth when you talk to me

*　　*　　*　　*

FOUND SOME!

*　　*　　*　　*

Without the chalkboard Woody is nothing

*　　*　　*　　*

Without Tony this show is something

*　　*　　*　　*

I prefer Fat Tuesday over Super Tuesday

*　　*　　*　　*

Yes, I want guacamole! (I know it costs extra)

*　　*　　*　　*

You're welcome, chalkboard industry

*　　*　　*　　*

Now might be a good time to buy stock in chalk

*　　*　　*　　*

I don't just bring meat, I bring Kobe beef

*　　*　　*　　*

I like my steak tartare well done

*　　*　　*　　*

I fish; therefore I lie

*　　*　　*　　*

I have a revolutionary new invention: the iPaige

*   *   *   *

iPaige movies are in 8D!

*   *   *   *

There's no "we" in iPaige

*   *   *   *

The iPaige plays 45 and 78 records (in stereo)

*   *   *   *

Don't confuse me with facts;
my mind's already made up

*   *   *   *

It's never too late to mutate

*   *   *   *

This would be really funny
if it weren't happening to me

*   *   *   *

They told me I had type-A blood,
but that was a typo

*   *   *   *

3

The question always is: "*Where* do you get the chalkboard quotes?"

Here's the answer: everywhere.

Jason Weindruch and I think up a lot of them. Jason has been my associate and production assistant since we began the show. He joined me soon after graduating in communications from Regis University in Denver. Before being hired, his job was to tape Catholic mass to replay for shut-ins at nursing homes. So he was experienced in dealing with someone like me. Jason has great penmanship, which is the most important quality for the blackboard. I have lousy penmanship, but I can spell. He can't. Like most young people, Jason grew up with spell-check. As

Hollywood Henderson of the Dallas Cowboys once said of Terry Bradshaw, Jason "couldn't spell 'cat' if you spotted him a c' and an 'a.'" Otherwise, he is an incredible man. Jason and I are a good team. We talk about chalkboard quotes every day. We really should get real jobs. In fact, Jason is. After 11 years, he is now planning a career in television. He wants to run NBC. 'So, tell us, Mr. Weindruch, why do you deserve this CEO job at a major network?' 'I've been doing chalkboard sayings for the past 11 years.' 'OK, you're hired.' Only Jason would write here, 'OK, *your* hired.' I've told him about 5,000 times the difference between *your* and *you're*. He doesn't get it. But he gets chalkboards.

Viewers have sent in hundreds of chalkboard sayings they've come up with or seen on bathroom walls or something. Some of mine come from bumper stickers, T-shirts, signs in diners, twists on famous quotes written by Benjamin Franklin, quotation books from the past 100 years, friends, relatives, people I meet on the street and in bars, some tourists I talk to in Hawaii and Mexico while on vacation and a waitress in a restaurant yesterday.

"I watch the show every day," the wait person said. "How about this quote: *Where are we going, and why am in this basket?*" I said sure.

So Jason and I were sitting in Bubba Gump's debating the meaning of her quote. He thought it had to do with a baby in a carriage. "No," I said. "I think it's what Toto might have said if he could talk in *Wizard of Oz*."

When the waitress returned, I asked her. "Oh, that's a reference to 'to hell in a hand basket.'" Makes sense. A lot of them do not. We don't try to make people think about the sayings. We're just having fun. They aren't meant to be serious or philosophical. They were just meant to entertain or take attention away from my stupidity for a few seconds.

Jason Weindruch gave himself the title of 'Remote Production Associate Producer Rocky Mountain' or something like that. How did he get a dream job working in sports television? I don't know. He applied. He had worked some behind the camera for the local public education channel. So he knew production, and he understood cameras and the technical side of the business, and all that stuff that is scattered all over our small studio in Denver. We have a prop closet that includes everything from a doctor's coat to a Star Wars battle helmet to a Slippery Rock football jersey. I asked Jason two questions the first day: "How old are you?" and "What do you want to accomplish in life?" He wouldn't answer the first. Years later I asked why.

"I was only 22, and I didn't want you to think I was too young for the job." What job? I didn't know what his job was and I didn't care how old he was. I became a columnist for a major newspaper at 24. I know young.

His second answer was, "I want to work in sports televison full time. That's my goal."

I said, "Well, I'll help you get there." He's been like chewing gum on my shoe ever since.

When I was offered an opportunity to go to New York and do a show, I declined. I didn't want to live in New York City, and I didn't want to get up early for an 8 A.M. show. My brain doesn't start working until about 10 A.M., and I didn't want to get up at 6:30 or so every day. Little did I know until I got to New York that it was demanded I arrive at the studio at 4 A.M. daily. I never would have taken that job at any price.

As it was, I made some serious demands.

First: money, of course. New York is the most expensive place in America.

Second, I wanted a car and driver, because I've always been told TV and movie stars have a car and driver.

Third, I wanted an apartment next to Central Park, because that's where Woody Allen and those rich and famous people lived, and that's where they filmed *Ghostbusters*. I ended up living about half a block from the apartment building featured in the movie. I had no ghosts, but there was slime on the street.

Fourth, I wanted Brooks Brothers to clothe me. Why? When Brooks Brothers came to Denver, I went shopping in the store to buy a suit because I always believed you were nothing until you drank expensive Scotch and wore a Brooks Brothers suit (I hate Scotch). I wore my usual outfit; jeans and a sweatshirt. Nobody would wait on me. Salespeople avoided me as if I stunk. Maybe I did. I finally realized an hour later they had decided I wasn't a Brooks Brothers kind of guy. So I would prove them wrong in New York. The store agreed to provide my clothes; about 25 suits, 10 pair of shoes, 300 ties (most still have the tags on them) and maybe 150 shirts. Nice.

Fifth, I demanded a dressing room with a small refrigerator and two Diet Cokes and a fruit plate every morning. True story. Network people still circulate the memo that nobody was allowed to eat the fruit plate because it was for "the star" (the memo was sarcastic). Other people who worked at the show ate the fruit plate every morning.

Sixth, I wanted green M&Ms. What an idiot! Yes, but I'd heard that rock stars demanded green M&Ms in their dressing rooms at concerts. I could imagine a roadie somewhere picking out all the other colors of M&Ms. It was my idea of a joke. I learned later that a rock band put that clause in contracts to assure that promoters would read the entire document. If there were no green M&Ms in the dressing room, the rock stars knew the promoter wasn't paying attention. Never got green M&Ms. Instead, I got cold pizza every day. Seriously.

And, finally, I requested that Jason, Cato to the Green Hornet, be hired as my assistant in New York because I wanted to fulfill his objective of working fulltime for the network.

I got a call from the producer who wanted to know if Jason was a sports expert. I said, "Of course he is. He knows everything about sports." She said the network only hired sports experts.

Two weeks after I started in New York, the producer called me into her office and closed the door. "You lied," she said.

"No I didn't. What are you talking about?"

"Jason knows nothing about sports. He doesn't even know who the Yankees are."

I replied: "Uh ..."

Jason knows who the Yankees are now but not much else about sports. He knows about most everything else, and he's always been in charge of the props. He wears a gorilla costume on the air sometimes, he can do research faster than anybody else I know, and he's up on all things pop culture. He's very, very smart and savvy even though he wouldn't know where to put a comma or a semi-colon if his career depended on it. But he's the best.

*   *   *   *

Back to the question of where I get my quotes: as Bob Costas said, I know cocktail napkins. I sit in bars while on the road and write chalkboard quotes all over bar napkins. People ask, "What are you doing?" "Oh, just writing blackboard quotes. I sell drywall." I really do have business cards my friends Al and Tory gave me that state 'Woody's Wholesale Drywall Service.' When somebody in a bar asks me what I do, I give them the card and tell them I can get them drywall—wholesale. That pretty much shuts down the bar conversation. It never seemed to serve well as a pickup line, either.

I got several chalkboard sayings from a store window in Key West and from another in Lahaina, Maui, from stuff Winston Churchill and Thomas Jefferson might have written on their own chalkboards, from books like *Hilarious Roasts, Toasts and One-Liners* by Gene Perret (*I told my mother my house was her house, and she sold it*) and hundreds of other sources, variations of lines I've seen in factories and on car bumpers, and from fellow passengers on airplanes who want to help. One email correspondent would write me chalkboard sayings every week for a few years. Then, he or his ideas died.

The world is a chalkboard quote. I'll take a line from Ben Franklin like "A stitch in time saves nine" and change it to, "A switch in limes saves time" and then I look at it, and say, "That sucks," and we won't use it.

I always think the bumper sticker, '*My son is an honor student at (Blank) High School*' is somewhat ludicrous (I know the parents are proud), so Jason and I turned it into '*My blackboard is smarter than your honor student.*' A lot of them are spontaneous; depending on the show and the subjects we're talking about that day, who the other panelists are, the sports news of the day, or just whatever is on my mind, or Jason's.

One day we were talking about blackboard quotes (as we do all the time) and Jason said "How about this one?" and I said "I don't get it." He told me I was stupid, and I agreed, and we used his saying, and I still don't know what it means. What do you think? *Some days you eat the bear, and some days the bear eats you.*

I wanted to change it to, *Some days you eat the bear, but don't count on it* or *Some days you eat the bear, but most days you can depend on the bear eating you* or *Some days you eat the bear, and some days the bear makes you eat the dirt.*

That's how it works. John Bartlett, who was responsible for *Bartlett's Familiar Quotations*, probably wouldn't be proud. But where did he get his quotes, and aren't some of them awful, too?

Sometimes, when I'm on the road sitting in a bar, I just start writing down possible blackboard sayings on the napkins while drinking Jack Daniel's and Diet Coke (no fruit plate).

One of the quotes I wrote on a napkin was this one about Tim Cowlishaw because I owed him. Tim, a long-time columnist for *The Dallas Morning News* and author of the poignant book *Drunk On Sports* actually has become one of my closest friends, along with Bill Plaschke, so I pick on them.

*   *   *   *

My dog could score more points than Tim
Cowlishaw on this show

*   *   *   *

I'm the "P" in ESPN

*   *   *   *

There's an "I" in Paige for a reason

*   *   *   *

You can't spell "ESPN" without "PENS"

*   *   *   *

I'm reading a book about anti-gravity
I just can't put it down

*   *   *   *

My ears keep ringing; I keep trying to answer

*   *   *   *

I was reading a book about the history of glue,
and it's sticking with me

*   *   *   *

Cowlishaw didn't like his beard at first
Then it grew on him

*   *   *   *

I did a theatrical performance about puns.
It was a play on words

*   *   *   *

Chuck Norris frequently donates blood to the
Red Cross. Just never his own

*   *   *   *

I'd like to help you out
Which way did you come in?

*   *   *   *

Today! Woody Paige unplugged

*   *   *   *

Show me an ATH loser,
and I'll show you Bill Plaschke

*　　*　　*　　*

I don't deserve this award, but I have arthritis and
I don't deserve that, either

*　　*　　*　　*

Humans are the only creatures that allow their
children to come back home

*　　*　　*　　*

Don't tell me the sky is the limit when there are
footprints on the moon

*　　*　　*　　*

Horse sense is the good judgment which keeps
horses from betting on people

*　　*　　*　　*

Happiness is having a large, loving, close-knit
family in another city

*　　*　　*　　*

There are 3 kinds of people in this world. Those
who can count and those who can't

*　　*　　*　　*

Beauty is a light switch away

*　　*　　*　　*

When it comes to thought,
some people stop at nothing

*　　*　　*　　*

The optimist sees the donut,
the pessimist sees the whole

*　　*　　*　　*

Donuts: Is there anything they can't do?

*   *   *   *

Practice doesn't make perfect
Perfect practice makes perfect

*   *   *   *

Experience is what you get when you didn't get
what you wanted

*   *   *   *

Those who throw dirt only lose ground

*   *   *   *

Statistics prove that people who have the most
birthdays live the longest

*   *   *   *

Don't go chasing waterfalls,
because you might drown

*   *   *   *

Enough about me,
now tell me what you think of me

*   *   *   *

Change is good, but dollars are better

*   *   *   *

When life gives you lemons,
squeeze them in people's eyes

*   *   *   *

Everyone hates me because I'm paranoid

*   *   *   *

I stopped fighting my inner demons;
we're on the same side now

*   *   *   *

Everyone is gifted. Some open the package sooner

*   *   *   *

If you can't see the bright side of life,
polish the dull side

*   *   *   *

I would never die for my beliefs because
I might be wrong

*   *   *   *

My friend David lost his ID so we call him Dav

*   *   *   *

Never forget a friend,
especially one who owes you money

*   *   *   *

has someone seen my capslock key?

*   *   *   *

Myspacebuttonisbroken

*   *   *   *

Who first put the alphabet in alphabetical order?

*   *   *   *

Cheer up, the worst is yet to come

*   *   *   *

The road to success is always under construction

*   *   *   *

Don't feel bad; I don't like me, either

*   *   *   *

The noblest of dogs is the hot dog;
it feeds the hand that bites it

*   *   *   *

Spoiler alert: Cowlishaw is first cut

*   *   *   *

The first cut on *Around The Horn* is the deepest;
the second cut hurts worse

*   *   *   *

Hey, I found your nose.
It was in my business again

*   *   *   *

Man dreads fame as a pig dreads fat

*   *   *   *

Know a good chemistry joke? Let me zinc about it

*   *   *   *

When chemists die, they barium

*   *   *   *

Broken pencils are like Jemele Hill: Pointless

*   *   *   *

I'd rather play Twister with myself

*   *   *   *

England has no kidney bank,
but it does have a Liverpool

*   *   *   *

Never trust a skinny chef

*   *   *   *

Never trust a naked bus driver

*   *   *   *

I used to be a banker, but I lost interest

*   *   *   *

Haunted French pancakes give me the crepes

*   *   *   *

I got a job at a bakery because
I kneaded the dough

*   *   *   *

I tried to catch some fog, but I mist

*   *   *   *

Venison for dinner again? Oh deer!

*   *   *   *

Velcro: What a rip off!

*   *   *   *

Jokes about German sausage are the wurst

*   *   *   *

I ♥ working nights and weekends and holidays.
I hate working the rest of the time

*   *   *   *

WARNING: He's subject to spontaneous
outburst of song

*   *   *   *

I'm not getting old, I'm getting awesome!

*   *   *   *

Middle age is when your age starts
to show around your middle

*   *   *   *

If you can't live without me,
why aren't you dead yet?

*   *   *   *

4

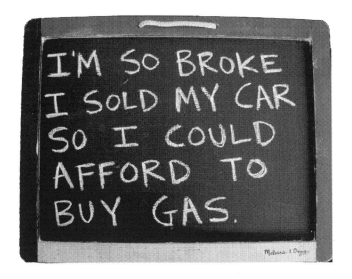

I never intended to become a television star, and of course, I'm not one. I'm not the driver of a clown car, but I play one on network TV.

I've wanted to be a writer, though, since I was 7, which was when my words first appeared in print, and, oddly enough, when I first appeared on a television show.

My second grade teacher, Mrs. Wood (true) at Cherokee Elementary asked me to write the class news for "The Cherokee Chit-Chat," a mimeograph newspaper for the school. She said I was the only kid in the class who actually could spell, a prerequisite, I suppose.

So I wrote about the new fish bowl we had in our classroom, and how we fed the goldfish every day. I also interviewed one of my classmates- a girl I thought was pretty. Very scintillating and newsworthy. When the newspaper came out, there was my story with my first byline. Several of the other boys and girls brought up the story during lunch period, and a couple laughed at me. That's exactly when I decided I was going to become a famous writer instead of a fireman.

Should have become a fireman.

I took my lunch money and bought a book for $1.99 entitled "Teach Yourself To Type." Only problem was, I didn't have a typewriter. But, at the back of the book was a cardboard sheet, with a fake keyboard, that you could cut out and fold out.

For several weeks I practiced typing on the cardboard. Eeeeee, iiiiii, ooooo, ppppp. Doesn't sound like much fun, but it sure beat those tap-dancing lessons my mother was making me take. I was the only boy in the afternoon class. I would have preferred playing football and baseball and basketball, and fighting with my best friend, Joey Bushwald.

Anyway, I learned how to type. I also took typing in high school, and, like tap-dancing, I was the only boy in the class, but I aced it, although, to this day, I have problems with the : and the ;.

Santa, or my parents, gave me an actual typewriter when I was in the fifth grade. It was a blue portable Olivetti. I used it for the next 20 years. I loved that typewriter. When I was covering sports and traveling for The Commercial Appeal in Memphis, I typed thousands of words on Old Blue. On the way home from a basketball trip, I checked the typewriter, which I never did. When I got back, it was broken in about 50 pieces. Thank you, baggage handlers. Goodbye, Old Blue.

In the seventh grade I was joke editor (true) for the Graceland Gazette, and every month I'd write about 12 jokes. Maybe that adventure led eventually to the chalkboard sayings.

Back to the second grade. My mom announced that I was going on the local TV show (in black and white; there was no color or high definition in 1953). The show was called "Storyland," and was hosted by Trent Wood (really) and was sponsored by a local dairy. I was one of a half-dozen kids who would listen to stories, watch some magic and sweat (because of the powerful TV lights and the lack of air-conditioning). My job was to taste the dairy's ice cream and proclaim it the best ice cream in the whole world.

Because of the heat in the studio, mashed potatoes were substituted for the ice cream, which would have melted like the wicked witch. "Oh, this is the greatest ice cream in the whole world," I said while thinking, 'These are the worst mashed potatoes in the whole world.'

A year later I was on another show on another station. Our neighbor was a camera man and he took his son and me to the Saturday morning show sponsored by a hot dog company. The show featured Laurel & Hardy serials. In between the hosts would talk about the great hotdogs, and the two boys would eat a hot dog (cold).

Side note- as an adult, while doing a morning show in New York, I was accused by a sports website of eating dog food live on the air. To set the record straight, I was eating potted meat (a luncheon product of unknown background) which is, I believe, worse than dog food.

Seems like I'm always eating on TV. In the past 12 years in front of the chalkboard, I've eaten hot dogs (to celebrate that July 4th contest at Coney Island), fried chicken (in honor of the Red Sox who ate Popeye's Chicken and drank beer in the clubhouse during games) and assorted cakes and Twinkies. Now you know how that all started.

For my appearance on the Saturday morning show, I got a wiener stuffed with $5 worth of quarters. My first paying gig on television.

When I was 10, I was booked by my stage mother (apparently) to be on "Mars Patrol" on WHBQ in Memphis. This is the same mother who made me a clown outfit and painted a washing machine carton blue, and had me be a Jack-In-The-Box in the Cotton Carnival parade. I guess that led to me being a clown as an adult. I should have been in therapy as a kid.

"Mars Patrol" was an afternoon program that showed "Buck Rogers" serials. Rogers was a futuristic space hero who fought bad guys from other planets. The set for our program was a very weak-looking space ship, and the camera man would zoom in on the five kids as if we were traveling at warp speed (this was long before Star Trek and Star Wars. I was an early day Luke Skywalker).

The captain of the ship and the host of the program was, in real life, a college student at Memphis State. His name was Wink Martindale. If he sounds somewhat familiar, Wink should. He went on to become a network game show host (Tic-Tac-Dough and many others) for decades, and still is alive (he was born in 1934) and doing occasional game shows from L.A. He wore a costume you wouldn't wish on your worst enemy. He looked somewhat like Captain Kirk with wings on his shoulder. We all had ray guns, and when you pulled the trigger, the barrel had a red light.

Little did Wink and Woody know they would end up on network TV from this little show.

But, wait. I'm not through with Wink. He would soon host a daily American Bandstand-type show called "Top Ten Dance Party." Guess who was on the show? Yes, I was. But that's not who I'm talking about. Elvis came in one day, leaned for about 45 minutes on the jukebox and talked about his latest movie and album. I wasn't there that day, though.

When I was a freshman in high school, my mother would drive me and a neighbor, Patty Widener, to "Top Ten…" or a competing show, "Big Beat," to dance in front of the camera with other couples. Don't ask me why I was doing it. I just went along with the concept. My mother must have figured out this would be great training for my future in sports television. She is the same mother who I brought to New York City when I was doing a daily two-hour live show every day, and said to me, "Can you take me to The Today Show?" She watches me now on TV, except when Dr. Phil has good guests, or she's playing Rummicube at the retirement home.

My dad, who died in his 40s (maybe out of his shame for me) never brought up the TV show I was on. He seemed more interested in my basketball, baseball and football games. Sadly, he never got to see me be a clown and eat food and have blackboard sayings on TV.

On "Big Beat" I was to judge new records. "I give it a 98 because it's easy to dance to, and it has a good, big beat." There I was telling stories again. Patty and I actually got a couple of cards from viewers saying we could dance well. Must have been those tap-dancing lessons.

At 13, I believed I was washed up on television.

* * * *

Tim Cowlishaw has the answer to everything and
the solution to nothing

* * * *

Bill Plaschke is too slow to keep worms in a tin

* * * *

Pick Mariotti's brain? I'd rather pick my nose

* * * *

ESPN pays Reali by the mute;
there had to be some reason

* * * *

Do computers cough when they get a virus

* * * *

I either get what I want, or I change my mind

* * * *

Do you put salt and powdered cheese
on popcorn shrimp?

* * * *

I only work to enjoy when I'm not working

* * * *

One drop of ink may make a million think

* * * *

You can't be late until you show up

* * * *

Prague: Czech it out

* * * *

Wyoming: There are no escalators

*   *   *   *

If you can't be a muse, at least be amusing

*   *   *   *

Canada: America's hat

*   *   *   *

Come to the dark side; we have cookies

*   *   *   *

Do as you're told, unless I tell you otherwise

*   *   *   *

I am a purfectionist

*   *   *   *

Three of us are wrong,
and the other has a blackboard

*   *   *   *

Life is only a test, and I have failed

*   *   *   *

There is a time and a place for everything
It is called Around The Horn

*   *   *   *

I am trying to imagine you with a personality

*   *   *   *

I suck, but my clone is awesome

*   *   *   *

Young once, immature forever

*   *   *   *

I forget why I'm here

*   *   *   *

I'm sorry you have to see me like this

*   *   *   *

I apologize. I'm sorry you have me confused with
someone who gives a damn what you think

*   *   *   *

Only elephants should wear ivory

*   *   *   *

Slippery as an eel in wolf's clothing

*   *   *   *

It wasn't me; it was the gorilla

*   *   *   *

I love mankind; it's people I don't like

*   *   *   *

My favorite animal is steak

*   *   *   *

Never eat more than you can lift

*   *   *   *

I was an extra on BayWatch

*   *   *   *

I'm not a doctor; I just play one on TV
Call me Dr. Fill

*   *   *   *

You get what you pay for in life
if you have nothing

*   *   *   *

Hurry up, pigeon.
I'm late for the early-bird special

*   *   *   *

Where facts are few, experts are many

*   *   *   *

I'm the world's leading authority
on Sears Catalogues

*   *   *   *

I know Victoria's secret

*   *   *   *

Coup de grass: Lawn mower

*   *   *   *

I'm happy; don't screw it up by talking to me

*   *   *   *

Thumb-wrestling champion

*   *   *   *

I have the body of a God. Buddha

*   *   *   *

Saliva drools, don't you think?

*   *   *   *

2 rules 4 success
1. Don't tell everybody everything you know
2.

*   *   *   *

1 out of 5 dentists recommends *Around the Horn.*
The other 4 recommend toothpaste

*   *   *   *

This blackboard quote looked better on paper

* * * *

Circular reasoning does not work
with square minds

* * * *

I didn't hear Mariotti; I was too busy being right

* * * *

Help me help you, Tony

* * * *

Dating Madonna exclusively

* * * *

I know I came here for something, but I forgot
what it was, so it must not have been important,
or maybe it wasn't, and what the hell

* * * *

Aibophopia: The fear of palindromes

* * * *

I came to chew gum and think. I'm all out of gum
and thoughts. What do I do now?

* * * *

In time we will look back on this show, discuss its
meaning and quickly change the subject

* * * *

I'm a rock star in the Republic of Rutabaga

* * * *

A pessimist is what an optimist calls a realist

* * * *

Think; perish the thought

*　　*　　*　　*

Hold the pepperoni and the paparazzi, please

*　　*　　*　　*

When in doubt, scream and run in circles; you feel
better, and you will have exercised

*　　*　　*　　*

Silence is not only tolerated here, but demanded

*　　*　　*　　*

Watch for my new cooking show:
Everybody Loves Ramen

*　　*　　*　　*

If I look lost and confused please
return me to Around The Horn

*　　*　　*　　*

Escalators don't break; they become stairs

*　　*　　*　　*

Pobody's Nerfect

*　　*　　*　　*

I'm a professional celebrity

*　　*　　*　　*

Wrong hurts; ask the other 3 panelists

*　　*　　*　　*

Mariotti is a slang word meaning "second place"

*　　*　　*　　*

I don't think much; there, I might be

*　　*　　*　　*

Talk only if you can do it silently

*   *   *   *

You are down to Earth,

but not quite far down enough for me

*   *   *   *

Don't go away mad. Stay and be mad, but just
shut up, or you'll make me mad, and I'll go away

*   *   *   *

When a door is open, it's ajar.

When a jar is open, is it adoor?

*   *   *   *

Dear IRS: Please cancel my subscription

*   *   *   *

Always proof read carefully

so you don't words out

*   *   *   *

March Madness takes its toll;

please have exact change

*   *   *   *

The information went data away

*   *   *   *

Don't be so open-minded; your brains will fall out

*   *   *   *

I have a degree in liberal arts …

do you want fries with that burger?

*   *   *   *

I don't listen when I talk in my sleep

*   *   *   *

5

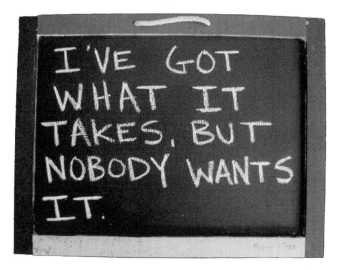

Now, back to how I ended up being in television. But first, that was the greatest ice cream in the world, and I give it a 98. And did I mention those good hot dogs?

As a student at the University of Tennessee, I was working on three potential careers; radio, television and newspapers. I wrote a daily column for the UT Daily Beacon; I did a radio show called "Woody Wakeup" and set a radio marathon record for being on the air for 104 hours, and I did an interview show for the campus TV station. I could manage to be bad at three things at once.

When I eventually became a sportswriter (after being a cityside reporter) at the Memphis Commercial Appeal, and about the time my first typewriter died, I was asked by WMC-TV to come back to appear on the station (where I had been on Storyland and Big Beat). The station manager asked me to be the color commentator on Memphis Pros ABA basketball games.

The first one we did was from Jackson, Tenn., and was between Memphis and the Indiana Pacers. There was no rehearsal. They just told me to talk when I had something to say, and somebody stuck an IFB in my ear. That's the earpiece you see everbody wear on TV. I still do every day. I don't know what 'IFB' stands for, but I do know that producers and directors can talk to you through it.

But, back then, I had no clue what it was. When the play-by-play announcer asked me a question in our pre-game presentation about the centers, and I started to answer, somebody who sounded like God said to me from somewhere, "Talk for about two minutes, then send it to commercial." I stopped talking immediately and replied, "OK." The voice from on high said, "Don't talk to me. Talk about the game." I said, "OK." The play-by-play guy took the conversation away from me. During the commercial break, a director ran in from the production truck and said, "What are you doing? You can't talk back to me while you're on the air." I said, "Oh, that was you, I thought that was God talking to me." He then explained the IFB to me.

My career as a basketball analyst was short-lived.

But, in Denver, I did talk radio for about 25 years with 16 different radio stations (and was fired from a dozen); I was on a variety of TV shows about sports, including "Sports Hounds," which featured four sports media people talking about sports issues (sounds familiar). I worked locally for channels 2, 4, 7, 9 and 53 and I was fired by channels 2, 4, 7, 9 and 53 and Fox Sports Rocky Mountain. When I asked one executive about the show I was doing, he said, "I'm indifferent." That show didn't last long. On 53 I did a Charlie Rose kind of one-on-one interview show with a famous athlete or coach. It was mainly a religious channel that showed old Western series. The manager came to me after six months and said, "We can make more money with a preacher or a cowboy than we can with you. You're off the air." Channel 2 fired me after I was sued by an indoor soccer player. He lost the lawsuit; I lost the show. I was doing nightly commentaries on Channel 7 news when I was asked by the general manager to become sports director and anchor. I declined until the money got rather ridiculous ($1.6 million for four years, and free suits). I signed a contract, and a press conference was scheduled for the next day. That morning the news director called me and said the press conference was off. The general manager had been fired. There will be a new general manger coming from Indianapolis the next week, and he wanted to meet with me.

When I walked into the office of the new GM, he didn't get up, which should have been a warning. He said he didn't want me as a sports director and anchor. He said he didn't want me as a commentator, either. I think part of it had to do with my attitude. When the old general manager asked me for suggestions for the slogan of 7 News, I replied, "Well, Channel 4 is We're 4 Denver, and Channel 9 is 9 Who Cares, I think, based on my year and a half there, your slogan should be Channel 7, If it's News, it's News to us."

An executive at Channel 9 told me I was too raw around the edges to continue to be on TV.

"I can do ice cream commercials."

*　　*　　*　　*

Be alert. The world needs more lerts

*　　*　　*　　*

Why, yes I am always this loud

*　　*　　*　　*

Lil Wayne Meet Bigg Woody

*　　*　　*　　*

Who's your edamame?

*　　*　　*　　*

Nobody should be this cool

*　　*　　*　　*

The 4th Jonas Brother

*　　*　　*　　*

Song of the decade: Hotplay's "Viva La Woody"

*　　*　　*　　*

Katy Perry wants to kiss me, and she'd like it

*　　*　　*　　*

Chalkboard Winter Tour '09 moves from Tampa
to Miami to Fiji

*　　*　　*　　*

Super Bowl Chimes for Big Ben & Me

*　　*　　*　　*

Gulls and boys together

*　　*　　*　　*

Hurry up, Tony, my yacht is double-parked

*　　*　　*　　*

Blackboard's got on its SPF 130

*   *   *   *

Chalkboard picked up a cardboard at the bar

*   *   *   *

Super Bowl XLII Super Drow LXII

*   *   *   *

Beware of irritable seagulls!

*   *   *   *

FILTHY STINKING RICH
(2 out of 3 ain't bad)

*   *   *   *

My 401-K is now a 101-K

*   *   *   *

I get enough exercise just pushing my luck

*   *   *   *

I jog my mind and run my mouth

*   *   *   *

Amnesia used to be my favorite word,
but then I forgot it

*   *   *   *

When I die, I'm leaving my body to science fiction

*   *   *   *

ATH: I do it for the yelling

*   *   *   *

Procrastinate now. Don't put it off

*   *   *   *

Do witches run spell checkers?

*   *   *   *

Exceptions always outnumber rules

*   *   *   *

Friends come and go, enemies accumulate

*   *   *   *

BUDGET: A method for
going broke methodically

*   *   *   *

Constant change is here to stay

*   *   *   *

DAIN BRAMAGED

*   *   *   *

If love is blind, why is lingerie so popular?

*   *   *   *

As long as I can remember, I've had amnesia

*   *   *   *

As I said before, I never repeat myself

*   *   *   *

A balanced diet is a cookie in each hand

*   *   *   *

I'm on the spit-it-out diet.
If the food tastes good, I spit it out

*   *   *   *

Why don't psychics win more lotteries?

*   *   *   *

Entering smug mode

*   *   *   *

Let the potato chips fall where they may

*   *   *   *

Never moon a werewolf

*   *   *   *

The cure for insomnia is more sleep

*   *   *   *

I never apologize, I'm sorry,
but that's the way I am

*   *   *   *

I know you are, but what am I?

*   *   *   *

According to my calculations
the problem doesn't exist

*   *   *   *

Adults are just kids who owe money

*   *   *   *

A splendid combination of talent and trouble

*   *   *   *

A PBS mind in an MTV world

*   *   *   *

I was uncool before uncool was cool

*   *   *   *

Don't insult an alligator
until you've crossed the river

*   *   *   *

I bet you I quit gambling years ago

*   *   *   *

Just be glad I'm not a twin

*   *   *   *

You have the right to remain silent. Tony Reali
will use anything you say to mute you

*   *   *   *

Just because I don't care
doesn't mean I don't understand

*   *   *   *

I'm out of my mind. Feel free to leave a message

*   *   *   *

Cogito ergo periculosus
(Translation: I think; therefore, I'm dangerous)

*   *   *   *

I drank a pint of varnish and got all lacquered up

*   *   *   *

I'm very assertive. I think

*   *   *   *

For a minute there Tim almost bored me to tears

*   *   *   *

Do not disturb. Already disturbed

*   *   *   *

I know you are nobody's fool
You're everybody's fool

*   *   *   *

I have a foggy bottom

*   *   *   *

Why is there only one
US Monopolies Commission?

*   *   *   *

Washington schlepped here

*   *   *   *

Save the planet! Annoy 1 person at a time

*   *   *   *

I spent the night in Lincoln's bathroom

*   *   *   *

Jackie reminds me of the ocean—
she makes me see-sick

*   *   *   *

People say I have no taste, but I like Tony

*   *   *   *

Most of us live and learn. Tony just lives

*   *   *   *

Jay is no longer beneath my contempt

*   *   *   *

What's the latest dope besides you?

*   *   *   *

I like your approach; now, let's see your departure

*   *   *   *

March madness: another reason not to work

*   *   *   *

On the other hand, you have different fingers

*   *   *   *

Honk if you love peace … and quiet

*   *   *   *

I used to be a narrator for bad mimes

*   *   *   *

Everywhere is walking distance
if you have the time

*   *   *   *

Corduroy Pillows: They're making headlines!

*   *   *   *

I like to reminisce with people I don't know

*   *   *   *

My new movie: "Beverly Hills Flop"

*   *   *   *

HollyWoody
The new star on the chalk of fame

*   *   *   *

If you're like me, and I know I am …

*   *   *   *

Clones are people, two

*   *   *   *

62-year-old one owner needs parts
Make best offer

*   *   *   *

I'm proof that evolution can go in reverse

*   *   *   *

I've been called into the ESPN principal's office
in Bristol, CT

*   *   *   *

I put the fun in dysfunction

*   *   *   *

My house was burned down
by a stress relieving candle

*   *   *   *

If there's one thing I can't stand, it's intolerance

*   *   *   *

Why do we bake cookies & cook bacon?

*   *   *   *

Not afraid of heights—afraid of widths

*   *   *   *

My inferiority complex is not as good as Mariotti's

*   *   *   *

Really really really ol' blue eyes

*   *   *   *

Indecision is the key to flexibility

*   *   *   *

If it ain't broke, fix it until it is

*   *   *   *

Half the people in the world are below average

*   *   *   *

A day without sunshine is like, uh, night, duh

*   *   *   *

My reality check bounced

*   *   *   *

No one ever says "It's only a game"
when they're winning

*   *   *   *

I got hit because I failed to dodge a Dodge

*   *   *   *

6

In Indianapolis recently, I spent the afternoon before an NFL game hanging out at the Kurt Vonnegut Literary Museum—and bought the T-shirt. The best thing there was a letter he wrote back to a woman who wanted the famous American writer to correspond regularly with her. He wrote, 'I'm tired of writing, and I don't want to start writing to you now.'

He was the best. My daughter and I got the chance to hang out one afternoon and evening with Vonnegut years ago before he died. It was a bigger thrill for me than being with Mickey Mantle, who wasn't very nice, but had a great quote; "If I knew I was going to live this long, I'd have taken better care of my body."

Vonnegut would have made extraordinary blackboard sayings, such as; "True terror is to wake up one morning and discover that your high school class is running the country," and "I'm here to tell you we are on Earth to fart around, and don't let anybody tell you different."

Emile Zola, a French novelist and activist, also would have made a great panelist and blackboard guy, except you'd have to translate his words. "If you ask me what I came into this life to do, I will tell you; I came to live out loud." And "If I cannot overwhelm with my quality, I will overwhelm with my quantity."

I would love to have been on a segment with Vonnegut, Zola and Oscar Wilde, with God as the host.

*   *   *   *

I hate people who steal my ideas
before I think of them

*   *   *   *

If you choke a smurf, what color does it turn?

*   *   *   *

Matadors are backstabbers

*   *   *   *

Nurses call the shots

*   *   *   *

I make dirt look good

*   *   *   *

Don't just go away, go weigh

*   *   *   *

Brunette is the new blonde

*   *   *   *

I don't know karate, but I do know crazy

*   *   *   *

These are my Sunday go-to-meeting clothes

*   *   *   *

A cubicle is just a padded cell without a door

*   *   *   *

Dijon Vu—The same mustard as before

*   *   *   *

The Spanish Optometrist Club? Si

*   *   *   *

The Antiperspirant Club? Sure

*   *   *   *

Gamblers Anonymous Club? You bet!

*   *   *   *

If Barbie is so popular,
why do you have to buy her friends?

*   *   *   *

For sale: Parachute; failed only once in 10 jumps

*   *   *   *

What does the winner of a "Best Trophy"
competition get?

*   *   *   *

To err is human; to forgive is not company policy

*   *   *   *

Rain dance tonight, weather permitting

*   *   *   *

3M and Goodyear merged;
new company called mmmGood

*   *   *   *

Grey Poupon and Dockers merged;
new company called Poupon Pants

*   *   *   *

John Deere and Abitibi Price merged;
now called Deere Abi

*   *   *   *

Everyone has a photographic memory
Some just don't have film

*   *   *   *

If Fed Ex and UPS were to merge,
would they call it Fed Up?

*   *   *   *

38% of people stop looking for work
when they find a job

*   *   *   *

If you don't like the news, go out and make some

*   *   *   *

Bill: If I throw a stick, will you leave?

*   *   *   *

The Peter Pan Club? Would I join?
Never—Never

*   *   *   *

The Quarterback Club? I'll pass

*   *   *   *

The Yoko Club? Oh no

*   *   *   *

Not all men are annoying; some are dead

*   *   *   *

And your cry baby, whiny opinion today would be
what, Cowlishaw?

*   *   *   *

Do they ever shut up on your planet Cowlishaw?

*   *   *   *

The average chocolate bar has 8 insect legs in it

*   *   *   *

The average human eats 8 spiders in his lifetime
at night

*   *   *   *

It's illegal to catch mice without a hunting license
in Cleveland

*   *   *   *

Where there's a will, there's a family fight over it

*   *   *   *

Nothing is foolproof to a talented fool

*   *   *   *

Monday is an awful way to spend 1/7 of your life

*   *   *   *

Give me 30 minutes, and I'll give you 5 of my best

*   *   *   *

Sometimes I feel like a nut,
sometimes I feel like a doughnut

*   *   *   *

For every action there is an equal and
opposite criticism

*   *   *   *

Never hire a cleaning lady named Dusty

*   *   *   *

This blackboard quote submitted by captive
audience. He's in prison

*   *   *   *

Men should always aim high
Then you won't splash on your shoes

*   *   *   *

Nostalgia isn't what it used to be

*   *   *   *

Stressed spelled backwards is DESSERTS

*   *   *   *

Why are there interstate highways in Hawaii?

*   *   *   *

Why isn't phonetic spelled the way it sounds?

*   *   *   *

Do Lipton Tea employees take coffee breaks?

*   *   *   *

Where do people from Hawaii go on vacation?
Detroit?

*   *   *   *

When I want your opinion,
I'll remove the duct tape

*   *   *   *

Isn't it scary
that doctors call what they do "practice"?

*   *   *   *

Love may be blind
but marriage is a real eye-opener

*   *   *   *

I'd like to have more self-esteem,
but I don't deserve it

*   *   *   *

Under my gruff exterior lies a gruffer interior

*   *   *   *

A dog has an owner; a cat has a staff

*   *   *   *

New Program: Bowling for Spelunkers

*   *   *   *

Consciousness: The annoying time between naps

*   *   *   *

I wouldn't touch the metric system
with a 3.048m pole

*   *   *   *

Can vegetarians eat animal crackers?

*   *   *   *

Studying friction can be a drag sometimes

*   *   *   *

A seminar on time travel will be held
two weeks ago

*　　*　　*　　*

It's hard to make a comeback when you haven't
been anywhere

*　　*　　*　　*

Beat the 7 o'clock rush hour; don't go to work

*　　*　　*　　*

Karaoke is a Japanese word meaning "tone deaf"

*　　*　　*　　*

Artificial intelligence is no match
for natural stupidity

*　　*　　*　　*

My mind is like a steel trap—
rusty and illegal in 37 states

*　　*　　*　　*

What was the best thing before sliced bread?

*　　*　　*　　*

Everybody repeat after me:
"We are all individuals"

*　　*　　*　　*

Chatters more than a dolphin by a fish bucket

*　　*　　*　　*

When cheese gets a photo taken, what does it say?

*　　*　　*　　*

A clear conscience is usually the sign of
a bad memory

*   *   *   *

Here I am! What are your other two wishes?

*   *   *   *

Failure is not an option.
It's bundled with your software

*   *   *   *

If at first you don't succeed, redefine success

*   *   *   *

Confession is good for the soul,
but bad for your career

*   *   *   *

Red meat is not bad for you; Fuzzy green meat is

*   *   *   *

The following statement is true;
the previous statement was false

*   *   *   *

Hairier than Chewbacca dipped in Rogaine

*   *   *   *

What's the synonym for synonym?

*   *   *   *

Shops at EXTREMELY Old Navy

*   *   *   *

All I ask is a chance to prove
money can't make me happy

*   *   *   *

Follow your dreams, except for that one where
you're naked at work

*   *   *   *

Which one of these is the non-smoking lifeboat?

*   *   *   *

I had amnesia once—maybe twice

*   *   *   *

Those that forget the pasta
are doomed to reheat it

*   *   *   *

A journey of a thousand miles begins at the ATM

*   *   *   *

I can't get enough minimalism

*   *   *   *

Onomatopoeia sounds like what?

*   *   *   *

I like life. It's something to do

*   *   *   *

I don't need your attitude, I have my own

*   *   *   *

How is it possible to have a civil war?

*   *   *   *

Money is the root of all wealth

*   *   *   *

Don't judge a book by its movie

*   *   *   *

Welcome to TGIWoody's

*   *   *   *

Age is a very high price to pay for maturity

*   *   *   *

There's too much blood in my caffeine system

*   *   *   *

It is easier to get forgiveness than permission

*   *   *   *

A consultant is a man from out of town who
carries a briefcase with nothing in it

*   *   *   *

I do whatever my Rice Krispies tell me to

*   *   *   *

Have an adequate day!

*   *   *   *

I'm not shy—I'm studying my prey

*   *   *   *

I'm really easy to get along with
once people learn to worship me

*   *   *   *

I've had fun before. This isn't it

*   *   *   *

I'm not myself today. Maybe I'm you

*   *   *   *

I'm not obnoxious, I'm verbally challenged

*   *   *   *

I'm not being rude, you're just insignificant

*   *   *   *

I prefer to remain anomalous

*   *   *   *

I plead contemporary insanity

*   *   *   *

I try to make everyone's day a little more surreal

*   *   *   *

I will always cherish the initial misconceptions
I had about you

*   *   *   *

I was raised to be charming, not sincere

*   *   *   *

I'll try being nicer if you'll try being smarter

*   *   *   *

If all else fails lower your standards

*   *   *   *

If I promise to miss you, will you go away?

*   *   *   *

It's not who wins or loses, it's who keeps score

*   *   *   *

7

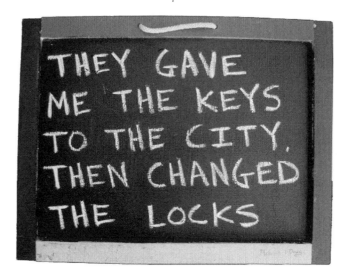

By now, this chapter should be self-explanatory. If not, move on to the next one.

*   *   *   *

Illiterate? Write me for help

*   *   *   *

I wish life had subtitles!

*   *   *   *

Me-topia better than utopia

*   *   *   *

I'm not cheap, but I am on special this week

*   *   *   *

If I agreed with you we'd both be wrong

*   *   *   *

Keep watching; I might do a good trick

*   *   *   *

Have you ever imagined a world without
hypothetical situations?

*   *   *   *

Can you buy an entire chess set in a pawn shop?

*   *   *   *

This is a day for firm decisions! Or is it?

*   *   *   *

I want patience—AND I WANT IT NOW!

*   *   *   *

Hard work never killed anyone, but why chance it?

*   *   *   *

If I want your opinion I'll have you fill out the
necessary forms

*   *   *   *

If a pig loses its voice, is it disgruntled?

*   *   *   *

Where do forest rangers go to get away from it all?

*   *   *   *

I hate to have a battle of wits
with an unarmed person

*   *   *   *

I look way better and am taller in person

*   *   *   *

My favorite mythical creature?
The honest politician

*   *   *   *

I was the imaginary friend for the kid next door

*   *   *   *

I saw Elvis. He sat between me and
Bigfoot on the UFO

*   *   *   *

Take my advice; I don't use it anyway

*   *   *   *

It is easier to get older than it is to get wiser

*   *   *   *

I'm not young enough to know everything

*   *   *   *

The early bird gets the worm
But the second mouse gets the cheese

*   *   *   *

I went to school to become a wit,
only made it halfway

*   *   *   *

Sometimes I need what only you can give me—
your absence

*   *   *   *

We got rid of the kids; the cat was allergic

*   *   *   *

Work fascinates me ... I could sit and
watch it for hours

*   *   *   *

Get the facts first; you can distort them later

*   *   *   *

If practice makes perfect,
how do you explain taxi drivers?

*   *   *   *

All the world's a stage;
I seem to have missed the rehearsal

*   *   *   *

Seen it all, done it all, can't remember most of it

*   *   *   *

I'm going to graduate on time,
no matter how long it takes

*   *   *   *

Gravity: It's not just a good idea. It's the law

*   *   *   *

Money talks, but all mine ever says is "Goodbye"

*   *   *   *

I wished the buck stopped here; I could use one

*   *   *   *

It's a small world. Unless you have to walk

*   *   *   *

For sale: Wedding dress. Size 10
Worn once by mistake

*   *   *   *

I'm going to start thinking positive,
but I know it won't work

*   *   *   *

Always wanted to be a procrastinator,
but never got around to it

*   *   *   *

I couldn't repair your brakes,
so I made your horn louder

*   *   *   *

Would a fly without wings be called a walk?

*   *   *   *

If a parsley farmer is sued,
can his wages be garnished?

*   *   *   *

Do people in Australia call the rest of the world
"up over"?

*   *   *   *

Anything is possible if you don't know what
you're talking about

*   *   *   *

I'm in shape. Round's a shape

*   *   *   *

Does killing time damage eternity?

*   *   *   *

I know it all,
I just can't remember it simultaneously

*   *   *   *

I have no intention of telling you my real name

*   *   *   *

I wanted a career;
turns out I just wanted a paycheck

*   *   *   *

We met in a past life,
and you were wrong then, too

*   *   *   *

I tried being reasonable once; I didn't like it

*   *   *   *

Macho law prohibits me from
admitting I'm wrong

*   *   *   *

Does your train of thought have a caboose?

*   *   *   *

Can I trade this job for what's behind door No. 1?

*   *   *   *

I'm writing a book.
I've got the page numbers done

*   *   *   *

Too many freaks, not enough circuses

*   *   *   *

I try to be modest, but I'm too great for that

*   *   *   *

Caution: I was not hired here for my disposition

*   *   *   *

More lightning round please!

*   *   *   *

Food is an important part of a balanced diet

*   *   *   *

Today's Show: 30 Rack

*   *   *   *

This is not an optical illusion;
it only looks like one

*   *   *   *

Don't eat clowns. They taste funny

*   *   *   *

Please, let me prove that winning the lottery
won't spoil me

*   *   *   *

I was not lying. I said things that later on seemed
to be untrue

*   *   *   *

The future will be better tomorrow

*   *   *   *

I can handle criticism so long as it isn't about me

*   *   *   *

I think that will take much longer than
I think it will

*   *   *   *

Solutions are not the answer to my problems

*   *   *   *

If your parents never had children,
chances are you won't, either

*   *   *   *

Fiction writing is great.
You can make up almost anything

*   *   *   *

If it weren't for electricity,
we'd all be watching ESPN by candlelight

*   *   *   *

Fool me once, shame on you
Fool me twice, prepare to die

*   *   *   *

Early morning cheerfulness can be
extremely obnoxious

*   *   *   *

I am free of all prejudices. I hate everyone equally

*   *   *   *

I HATE NEGATIVE PEOPLE!

*   *   *   *

Power Corrupts; absolute power is kind of neat

*   *   *   *

My life has a superb plot,
but I think I die at the end

*   *   *   *

I always smile cause
I have no idea what's going on

*   *   *   *

I'm not a complete idiot; some parts are missing

*   *   *   *

If you think education is expensive, try ignorance

*   *   *   *

Dear Auntie Em: Don't like you, hate Kansas,
taking the dog –Dorothy

*   *   *   *

I wanna live 'til I die, no more, no less

*   *   *   *

Just smile and nod; everyone will think
you know what's going on

*   *   *   *

Age only matters if you're cheese

*   *   *   *

There aren't enough days in the weekend

*   *   *   *

When in doubt, mumble

*   *   *   *

Don't hate yourself in the morning
Sleep until noon

*   *   *   *

He who throws dirt loses ground

*   *   *   *

Forget the health food
I need all the preservatives I can get

*   *   *   *

It's a small world, unless you have to clean it

*   *   *   *

Do radioactive cats have 18 half-lives?

*   *   *   *

If ignorance is bliss,
why is Kevin Blackistone so sad?

*   *   *   *

If you don't know what Evian is spelled backward,
you're naïve

*   *   *   *

If we quit voting will they all go away?

*   *   *   *

Aim low, reach your goals, avoid disappointment

*   *   *   *

Teamwork means never having to take
all the blame

*   *   *   *

The only true wisdom is in knowing
you know nothing

*   *   *   *

8

As I walked down the beach at the Mauna Kea resort on the Big Island of Hawaii, I saw a famous TV star: Kathleen Sullivan. She was co-host, with Harry Smith, of CBS This Morning. I approached and told her how much I always had respected her work and that Harry was a friend. He and I had worked at Channel 7 together, and he had been a DJ on a Denver radio station I worked for. We talked for a while, and she didn't seem very happy.

I thought if I were on network television, particularly on a morning show, I'd be the happiest person on Earth.

Not long after, Sullivan was taken off the morning show on CBS. Maybe, I thought, network TV isn't so great after all. By the way,

Sullivan has gone on to have a great career on TV and on the internet, and she was the first woman to co-host the Olympics.

Even though Smith eventually left the show, too, after a lengthy run, he has continued to be a distinguished network correspondent and commentator. I'm proud of him.

When I went to New York several years ago to join a morning show, I called Harry and left a message, asking for advice. He didn't return my call. But months later, I was sitting at an Italian restaurant across from Lincoln Center, and Harry approached with two young men. He introduced his sons and said they were fans.

They said they loved the blackboards.

"If you ever want to come watch a real morning show, or if you ever need advice, just call me."

Good to see you, Harry.

Somehow over the years, I was invited by networks to be on "Today," "Good Morning America," "Hannity and Colmes," "SportsCenter," and a dozen other sports shows and even CNN. I have a face for radio, a voice for newspapers. I always laughed. Who? Me? I was tap dancing as fast as I could.

In my 50s I realized I didn't want to be on radio or TV any more. I just wanted to write a column.

Then, along came a network TV show, and another, and another, and more shows. But I'll always have "Mars Patrol," where I learned about props and costumes.

Then along came the chalkboard, and these sayings.

*   *   *   *

Do band members like to play
Around The French Horn?

* * * *

Do seamstresses play Around the Torn?

* * * *

Did General Custer play Around the Big Horn?

* * * *

Do sailors play Around Cape Horn?

* * * *

Do pediatricians play Around the Born?

* * * *

Do Plaschke's friends play Around the Forlorn?

* * * *

Do wildebeest play Around the Horns?

* * * *

Do people from Nebraska play Around the Corn?

* * * *

Plz tell tony 2 stop texting me

* * * *

Same Blackboard, different day

* * * *

Brain loading, please wait ...

* * * *

I can't hear you over the sound of how right I am

* * * *

My entourage is on vacation

*   *   *   *

Tell me what you believe,
and I'll tell you where you're going wrong

*   *   *   *

Dorothy got lost in Oz because
3 men were giving her directions

*   *   *   *

A meeting is an event where minutes are taken
and hours are wasted

*   *   *   *

Meetings: The practical alternative to work

*   *   *   *

Even if the voices are not real,
they have some good ideas

*   *   *   *

Fewer bombs, more art supplies

*   *   *   *

The question is: Who are Tony Reali and
Alex Trebek, and why?

*   *   *   *

Ever stop to think and forget to start again?

*   *   *   *

I don't believe in miracles; I rely on them

*   *   *   *

I run with scissors

*   *   *   *

I took an I.Q. test, and the results were negative

*   *   *   *

My mind is wandering, and I can't find it

*   *   *   *

If wrong could fly, this show would be an airport

*   *   *   *

True wisdom is found on blackboards

*   *   *   *

Loud: just one more service I offer

*   *   *   *

I use pepper spray to spice up my steaks

*   *   *   *

Muffins are just ugly cupcakes

*   *   *   *

Help stop global whining

*   *   *   *

Will work because I have to

*   *   *   *

My brain has a mind of its own

*   *   *   *

I'm too pretty to do math

*   *   *   *

Careful, you'll end up in my next book

*   *   *   *

Jenius

*   *   *   *

I don't have an inside voice

*   *   *   *

My nickname is Justin. Justincredible

*   *   *   *

Don't tase me Tony

*   *   *   *

I've counted to infinity

*   *   *   *

Don't talk to me; I'm talking to myself

*   *   *   *

Even your poker face is ugly

*   *   *   *

Pillow talk costs extra

*   *   *   *

I'm the ESPN Employee of the Month. I wish

*   *   *   *

Frogger or Pacman?

*   *   *   *

Noogie patrol

*   *   *   *

I do my own nude scenes

*   *   *   *

Band Camp Rocks

*   *   *   *

I can resist everything except temptation

*   *   *   *

Don't make me call out my flying monkeys

*   *   *   *

I'm sorry. My fault
I forgot you were chump-change

*   *   *   *

No sense in being pessimistic;
It wouldn't work anyway

*   *   *   *

There is intelligent life on Earth,
but I'm just visiting

*   *   *   *

Life is not a cabaret. It's a dive bar

*   *   *   *

It is sad to grow old, but nice to ripen

*   *   *   *

End of decade but not end of decadence

*   *   *   *

A New Year's resolution is something that goes in
one year and out the other

*   *   *   *

Dear Santa, I can explain

*   *   *   *

I must confess; I was born at a very early age

*   *   *   *

Computers can accomplish things really fast,
like get you angry

*   *   *   *

A word to the wise isn't important
Words to the stupid matter

*   *   *   *

Don't know what your problem is,
but I bet it's difficult to pronounce

*   *   *   *

Everything that I can't find
I know is in a very secure place

*   *   *   *

The mind is like a parachute
It doesn't work unless it's open

*   *   *   *

I childproofed my house. But they still get in

*   *   *   *

The best things in life are not things

*   *   *   *

Criticizing is easy; stay tuned, and watch me do it

*   *   *   *

I don't need no educashun

*   *   *   *

I didn't escape; I got a day pass

*   *   *   *

The magician got so mad he pulled his hare out

*   *   *   *

Sea captains don't have crew cuts

*   *   *   *

A chicken crossing the road is poultry in motion

*   *   *   *

Gardeners who play baseball always know
the ground rules

*   *   *   *

With her marriage she got a new name and a dress

*   *   *   *

There are two types of people:
those who finish what they start and tho

*   *   *   *

I'm not lost; I just don't know
where I am or where I'm going

*   *   *   *

Always forgive your enemies;
nothing annoys them so much

*   *   *   *

Rumors go in one ear and out of many mouths

*   *   *   *

If at first you don't succeed, go to 2nd base

*   *   *   *

Who's on first? No, Who is the headline act?

*   *   *   *

Walk the walk; Talk the talk; Chalk the chalk

*   *   *   *

I'm starring in a remake of the movie
"Blackboard Jungle"

*   *   *   *

The two most common elements on this show are
hydrogen and stupidity

*   *   *   *

If love isn't a game,
then why are there so many players?

*   *   *   *

Research is what I'm doing when
I don't know what I'm doing

*   *   *   *

Wise men make proverbs, but fools repeat them

*   *   *   *

My homework is like steak—rare and
never well done

*   *   *   *

I'm not into working out
My philosophy: no pain no pain

*   *   *   *

Warning: Dates on calendar are closer
than they appear

*   *   *   *

Dust is a protective coating for fine furniture

*   *   *   *

Skipping school to bungee jump
will get you suspended

*   *   *   *

A boiled egg in the morning is hard to beat

*   *   *   *

Long fairy tales have a tendency to dragon

*   *   *   *

9

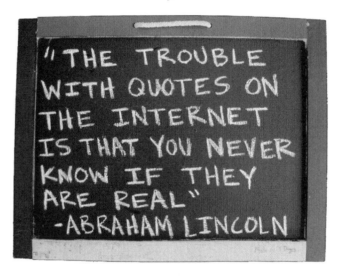

Abe Lincoln would have been much better at my job than I am. Except, I think it's tough to be a grown man with a chalkboard and expect to run for public office, or be any kind of success in life.

* * * *

If you can't be kind, at least be vague

* * * *

Do I get double points for my split personality?

* * * *

ATH would get higher ratings if
I were the only panelist

*   *   *   *

I use a stunt man for the tough questions

*   *   *   *

Big words don't scare me; using them does

*   *   *   *

I want to ask and answer my own questions

*   *   *   *

I have fan clubs in all 53 states and Texas

*   *   *   *

I speak 3 languages fluently
English is not one of them

*   *   *   *

Sarcasm is a body's natural defense
against stupidity

*   *   *   *

Kids adore me because
I'm not smarter than a 5th grader

*   *   *   *

Kids adore me because
I talk to my Rice Krispies, too

*   *   *   *

The early bird gets the worm
I'd rather sleep in and have pancakes

*   *   *   *

At my age middle of the night is 11 p.m.

*   *   *   *

Powerpoint presentations
have rendered me useless

*   *   *   *

I'm perfect unless you count my losses on this
show and my life

*   *   *   *

Wanna play hopscotch, or just drink Scotch?

*   *   *   *

If you can't do something right, do it yourself

*   *   *   *

I'm board, and hanging by a thread

*   *   *   *

Fishing is addictive. You can get hooked

*   *   *   *

My failures are only exceeded by my mistakes

*   *   *   *

I would score more points
if I understood the questions

*   *   *   *

I can beat Plaschke even when I'm not here

*   *   *   *

My crystal ball says the Ouija board is fake

*   *   *   *

How does non-stick coating stick to frying pans?

*   *   *   *

Don't eat the mussels in Brussels or the red beans
in New Orleans

*   *   *   *

Don't eat the turkey legs in Turkey
or at a deli in New Delhi

*   *   *   *

Don't eat the cow in Moscow
or the bull in Instanbul

*   *   *   *

Don't blame my teachers. They did the best they
could. They never had a chance

*   *   *   *

New year same old sh … ow

*   *   *   *

Not now arctic puffin!

*   *   *   *

I went to school before there was history to study

*   *   *   *

I never get my mix all talked up

*   *   *   *

My mediocre is better than Plaschke's best

*   *   *   *

I have a lot of time on my hands
when I wear two watches

*   *   *   *

I must have said it a million times,
I do not exaggerate

*   *   *   *

I wish to report the strange disappearance of
my hopes and dreams

*   *   *   *

Gnihtyreve smees drawkcab

*   *   *   *

I often quote myself;
it adds credibility to my argument

*   *   *   *

People who go camping are really intense

*   *   *   *

The best argument is that which seems
merely an explanation

*   *   *   *

Discussion is an exchange of knowledge;
argument an exchange of information

*   *   *   *

The person who sees both sides of a question,
sees nothing at all

*   *   *   *

When's Vice-Presidents Day?

*   *   *   *

Washington is the only President who didn't
blame the previous administration

*   *   *   *

Tony is either charming or tedious

*   *   *   *

Of all the animals,
Tony is the most unmanageable

*   *   *   *

I'm cooler than anyone not in a refrigerator

*   *   *   *

I never finish anyth

*   *   *   *

Zombies like me for my brain

*   *   *   *

Being awesome has its disadvantages

*   *   *   *

As a matter of fact,
the world does revolve around me

*   *   *   *

Just be glad I'm not your kid

*   *   *   *

Poets and pigs are only appreciated
after their deaths

*   *   *   *

I know karate and 2 other Japanese words

*   *   *   *

I'm not feeling myself today. This is my clone

*   *   *   *

Sorry about what happens later …

*   *   *   *

Any way we can speed this up?

*   *   *   *

For Sale: Host—Cheap

*   *   *   *

If I agree with Cowlishaw we both must be wrong

*   *   *   *

Buy one dog, get one flea

*   *   *   *

An expert farmer is outstanding in his field

*   *   *   *

If a tomato is a fruit,
does that make ketchup a smoothie?

*   *   *   *

I just got skylights put in my apartment
The people above me are furious

*   *   *   *

Never mess up an apology with an excuse

*   *   *   *

Tony should be issued a
Woody-to-English dictionary

*   *   *   *

A good pun is its own reword

*   *   *   *

I deserve a bye into the showdown every day

*   *   *   *

My two cents is worth a fortune in your currency

*   *   *   *

I have many, many moot mute points

*   *   *   *

Here's some good advice: Never take my advice

*   *   *   *

Those who think they know everything
annoy those of us that do

*   *   *   *

Sticks and stones may break my bones …
and it hurts

*   *   *   *

Bob Ryan writes his columns on an
Etch-A-Sketch

*   *   *   *

Can you tell I do daily brain exercises?

*   *   *   *

If you think my answers confuse you,
you should try being in my head for a day

*   *   *   *

I complement my flimsy arguments
with bad delivery

*   *   *   *

It's not whether you win or lose,
but how you place the blame

*   *   *   *

I'm never at a loss for words;
A coherent argument is another story

*   *   *   *

I only make up stats when I don't have facts

*   *   *   *

Normal people worry me

* * * *

Cleverly disguised as a responsible adult

* * * *

Violinists don't work; they just fiddle around

* * * *

I wear 2 watches
so I will have more time on my hands

* * * *

The sooner you fall behind,
the more time you'll have to catch up

* * * *

I didn't lose my mind; I sold it on ebay

* * * *

My NBA bracket is chalk suey

* * * *

It is not my fault that I never learned
to accept responsibility

* * * *

Suburbia: Where they cut down trees and
name streets after them

* * * *

Jemele Hill obviously is not king of the mountain

* * * *

If the entire world's a stage, I didn't get cast!

* * * *

10

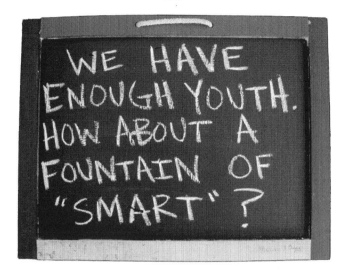

Tony Reali idolizes Alex Trebek, and wants to be the host of *Jeopardy*, to make his dad proud. Reali wrote the foreword to this book. He should have written the backward. This is a guy who once broke his finger using the 'mute' button, and said one day, "The two stars of this show are inanimate objects: the blackboard and the mute button." What do you expect? He's from Staten Island and graduated from Fordham.

*   *   *   *

Reali mutes ambidextrously,
but only scores with his right hand

*   *   *   *

What do sheep count
when they want to fall asleep?

*   *   *   *

Mediocrity is my comfort zone

*   *   *   *

Chalkboard doesn't pick chalk

*   *   *   *

Crazy is a relative term in my family

*   *   *   *

About as subtle as a flying brick

*   *   *   *

There's no future in time travel

*   *   *   *

Never look back unless
you're planning to go that way

*   *   *   *

Never kick a man when you're down

*   *   *   *

Nothing improves my memory more
than trying to forget

*   *   *   *

I thank my lucky stars I'm not superstitious

*   *   *   *

I never know how much of what I say is brilliant
or maybe Silly Putty

*   *   *   *

Diane Keaton once asked me out
I was in her room at the time

*   *   *   *

If you can't annoy somebody, there's little purpose
of being on this show

*   *   *   *

Criticism comes easier than craftsmanship

*   *   *   *

I'm proud to say I'm a humble person

*   *   *   *

The cure for writer's cramp is writer's block

*   *   *   *

Caution! Be careful of false, meaningless, and not
even very funny warnings, like this one

*   *   *   *

I had delusions of adequacy

*   *   *   *

Tony's barber must really hate him

*   *   *   *

When you come into a room
the mice jump on chairs

*   *   *   *

About as useless as a pulled tooth

*   *   *   *

Tim has an inferiority complex —
and it's fully justified

*   *   *   *

Failure has gone to his head

* * * *

I can't seem to remember your name,
but please don't help me

* * * *

Hard work pays off in the future;
laziness pays off now

* * * *

A good rooster crows in any hen house

* * * *

Top 10 reasons to procrastinate:
1. (I'll get back to you on that later)

* * * *

Experience is something you don't get
until after you need it

* * * *

I know so little, but I know it so fluently

* * * *

Double negatives are not a no-no

* * * *

Sometimes I mispell on perpose
Sometimes dolphins misspell on poipose

* * * *

I can't hear you over the sound of how epic I am

* * * *

I think outside the crate

* * * *

Stand Back! I'm a professional

*   *   *   *

I'm not good at empathy
Will you accept sarcasm?

*   *   *   *

Oh, look! Just 364,823 more days 'til
I start caring what you think

*   *   *   *

Delightfully tacky, yet unrefined

*   *   *   *

My cult-like following is
now accepting applications

*   *   *   *

Disinclined to play by the rules

*   *   *   *

I'm like a super hero, but with no powers or
motivation or comic book

*   *   *   *

Just pretend I'm not here. That's what I'm doing

*   *   *   *

I'd be a morning person
if it didn't start so early in the day

*   *   *   *

I'm sugar and spice and everything nice
If you wanna mess with me, you better think twice

*   *   *   *

Everyone in life has a purpose,
even if it's to serve as a bad example

* * * *

They say the truth will set you free
But I just keep getting muted

* * * *

I could skip the 1st round and
still beat today's panel

* * * *

Plaschke doesn't even know what
Facetime means

* * * *

Look up for inspiration, down for concentration,
at me for good information

* * * *

Reali gives Cowlishaw pity points

* * * *

Face Time should be: 1 second x winners age

* * * *

I didn't lose … I just ran out of wit

* * * *

I just wish my mouth had a backspace key

* * * *

I've only met four perfect people in my life,
and I didn't like any of them

* * * *

Here's a good idea ... uh ... I forgot

* * * *

New game plan ... cancel it

* * * *

Growing old is mandatory; growing up is sad

* * * *

I wouldn't do volunteer work if they paid me

* * * *

If you can remain calm,
you just don't have all the facts

* * * *

Buses travel faster
when you're outside running after them

* * * *

If you don't believe in love at first sight,
should I walk by again?

* * * *

I've got a problem for your solution

* * * *

There are no stupid questions;
except the ones on this show

* * * *

Don't be so humble. You're not that great

* * * *

"Be yourself" is the worst advice
you can give Plaschke

* * * *

I'm as strong as an ox and almost as intelligent

* * * *

Turn off the heat. The party is over

* * * *

My alarm clock doesn't ring. It applauds!

* * * *

The secret to looking young
is watching me on this show everyday

* * * *

Too many people give advice
when what you really need is a loan

* * * *

To get your kids attention,
stand in front of the TV

* * * *

The best things in life are free,
and so are the bad predictions on this show

* * * *

Everybody is somebody else's weirdo

* * * *

Well done is better than well-bred

* * * *

You guys pair up in groups of three,
then line up in a circle

* * * *

Predictions are difficult,
especially about the future

*　　*　　*　　*

I love California; I practically grew up in Phoenix

*　　*　　*　　*

A bachelor's life is no life for a single man

*　　*　　*　　*

Forget the Joneses!
I can't keep up with the Simpsons

*　　*　　*　　*

I love the great state of Chicago

*　　*　　*　　*

Always try to be modest, and remind everyone
you are

*　　*　　*　　*

By the time you find greener pastures,
you're too old to climb the fence

*　　*　　*　　*

No matter how late it is,
it's never as late as it will be later on

*　　*　　*　　*

Don't be surprised if someday I surprise you

*　　*　　*　　*

I like to study tourists in their native habitat

*　　*　　*　　*

I wish I could get a mirror with a better view

*　　*　　*　　*

For me, it would be very unusual
to have a usual day

*   *   *   *

Macho does not prove mucho

*   *   *   *

Read this, or you'll be sorry
On the other hand you may be sorry, anyway

*   *   *   *

Errors have been made. I will be blamed

*   *   *   *

I treasure every moment Plaschke is muted

*   *   *   *

A metaphor is a simile with attitude

*   *   *   *

At the end of the day … I go to sleep

*   *   *   *

11

Years ago, in the Al Pacino movie *Dog Day Afternoon*, his character robs a bank to get money for his boyfriend to have a sex-change operation. The bank in New York is surrounded by police, but Sonny Wortzik (Pacino) has several hostages and makes numerous demands, including a bus to the airport and a charter airplane bound for anywhere he chooses. Sonny asks his friend what foreign country he'd like to go to, and his reply is: "Wyoming."

I'm not particularly liked in such cities as Salt Lake City, Pittsburgh, Jacksonville, Tucson and several other cities, such as Nebraska. But I was asked to be the grand marshal of a Cheyenne Frontier Days Parade one year, and I've met a lot of nice people in Wyoming.

You should go sometime. Yellowstone is great. And the daddy of 'em all rodeo in Cheyenne allows adults to dress up like a cowboy.

I was born and grew up in Memphis, Tenn., and when I was a small boy, my family lived in Lauderdale Courts, a government housing project. Our neighbors were the Preseleys. They had a son named Elvis, and he used to play his guitar on the porch. My mother said he would "never amount to nothing." I think she actually was talking about me.

So I came up with a couple of blackboard sayings.

*   *   *   *

I'm kind of a minor deal in Wyoming,
especially in Laramie

*   *   *   *

Elvis is not dead; he lives down in my basement
and under an assumed name

*   *   *   *

This chalkboard is 100% organic

*   *   *   *

I used to have a fear of hurdles, but I got over it

*   *   *   *

Stop staring at me when I'm invisible!

*   *   *   *

A new type of broom came out;
it's sweeping the nation

*   *   *   *

I relish the fact that you've mustard
the strength to ketchup to me

*   *   *   *

If you want to recapture your youth,
just cut off his allowance

*   *   *   *

Anyone can win ATH, unless Tony is hosting

*   *   *   *

A yawn is a silent shout

*   *   *   *

Some folks are wise, and some otherwise

*   *   *   *

Coffee just isn't my cup of tea

*   *   *   *

Never argue with a fool
People might not know the difference

*   *   *   *

Imagine there were no hypothetical situations

*   *   *   *

Excuse me while I change
into something more formidable

*   *   *   *

Does the noise in my head bother you?

*   *   *   *

Why let reality or Reali wreck your day?

*   *   *   *

Born to run amuck

*   *   *   *

I've been watching TV wrong;
I always run to the fridge during commercials;
maybe I should run to the fridge between
commercials; that way I don't miss any

*   *   *   *

I'm so bored, I may resort to doing some work

*   *   *   *

So much to do, so few people to do it for me

*   *   *   *

Support your local planet!

*   *   *   *

A good sport has to lose it to prove it

*   *   *   *

I'm not in it to win it; I'm in it to spin it

*   *   *   *

I have a photographic memory that has never
been fully developed

*   *   *   *

Never let a computer know you're in a hurry

*   *   *   *

A man's home is his castle,
in a manor of speaking

*   *   *   *

The man who fell into an upholstery machine
is fully recovered

*   *   *   *

Once you've seen one shopping center,
you've seen 'emall

*   *   *   *

When two egotists meet, it's an I for an I

*   *   *   *

If you wish to live wisely, ignore sayings,
especially this one

*   *   *   *

The latest survey shows that 3 out of 4 people
make up 75% of the world's population

*   *   *   *

My favorite color is clear

*   *   *   *

Plaschke's favorite color is argyle

*   *   *   *

My 2nd favorite color is bloodshot eyes

*   *   *   *

The dead batteries were given free of charge

*   *   *   *

I mowed my yard last night:
it was a Coup De Grass

*   *   *   *

Dwn wth vwls

*   *   *   *

The chalkboard is the original Twitter

*   *   *   *

You can't judge a cover by its book

*   *   *   *

When it pours it rains

*   *   *   *

Just waking up … never seen a machine like
ATH … wow!

*   *   *   *

Hey Lil Wayne: I listen to your 3-peat;
now watch my 3-peat

*   *   *   *

Waste is a terrible thing to mind

*   *   *   *

Last guys finish nice

*   *   *   *

It's over til it's not over

*   *   *   *

Today is the tomorrow
you worried about yesterday

*   *   *   *

The gene pool could use a little chlorine

*   *   *   *

Too clever is dumb

*   *   *   *

Never turn your back on a charging turtle

*   *   *   *

The more you understand me, the crazier you get

*   *   *   *

I'm boldly going nowhere

*   *   *   *

I used to work in a blanket factory, but it folded

*   *   *   *

Never buy a car you can't push

*   *   *   *

The colder the x-ray table, the more of your body
is required on it, and exposed

*   *   *   *

The severity of the itch is
proportional to the reach

*   *   *   *

He who hesitates is probably right

*   *   *   *

Don't sweat petty things … or pet sweaty things

*   *   *   *

Two wrongs are only the beginning

*   *   *   *

He's about as useful as a trap door on a canoe

*   *   *   *

The bottom line is it's top drawer

*   *   *   *

I don't repeat gossip, so listen carefully

*   *   *   *

The best time to make friends
is before you need them

*   *   *   *

Some of my best friends are acquaintances

*   *   *   *

One's best friend is oneself

*   *   *   *

My face is unclouded by thought

*   *   *   *

Talk is cheap because supply exceeds demand

*   *   *   *

Ask me how I tolerate stupid questions

*   *   *   *

I'm so great I'm jealous of myself

*   *   *   *

I didn't say it was your fault;
I said I was blaming you

*   *   *   *

Go ahead and talk to me;
my day was ruined anyway

*   *   *   *

Without geography, you're nowhere

*   *   *   *

I'm about to have my next mood swing;
get out of my way

*   *   *   *

I give 100% 10% of the time

*   *   *   *

Asteroids rock!

*   *   *   *

Never test the depth of the water with both feet

*   *   *   *

I'm positive I lost an electron

*   *   *   *

How's my deriving?

*   *   *   *

Cancel my subscription, I'm tired of your issues

*   *   *   *

I'll bet you $500 I don't have a gambling problem

*   *   *   *

If you can read this,
you're within roundhouse kick range

*   *   *   *

Because roses are red,
violets are blue and depressed

*   *   *   *

WARNING! If zombies chase us,
I'm tripping you

*   *   *   *

Back in my day we had 5 planets

*   *   *   *

Hw do u kp a txtr in suspense? I'll tel u 2marO

*   *   *   *

A bad plan is better than no plan

*   *   *   *

Spelling is a lossed art

*   *   *   *

Always be sincere, even if you don't mean it

*   *   *   *

Do humpback whales recognize hump day?

*   *   *   *

Stay back 200 ft.
Not responsible for broken windshields

*   *   *   *

Hold your breath until I come back

*   *   *   *

Stand Back! I'm going to try science

*   *   *   *

Money talks; I'm too stupid to listen

*   *   *   *

What will be may be

*   *   *   *

2B or not 2B? That is the pencil

*   *   *   *

I'm not 65 today.
I'm $64.95 plus shipping and handling

*   *   *   *

Plaschke is too sexy for his hair,
that's why there's none there

*   *   *   *

I've never had premonitions,
but I think one day I might

*   *   *   *

Polynesia: Memory loss in parrots

*   *   *   *

Is "Tired old cliche" one?

*   *   *   *

Dust: mud with the juice squeezed out

*   *   *   *

Perforation is a rip-off

*   *   *   *

A friend is someone who's there
when he needs you

*   *   *   *

The best deals are the deals never made

*   *   *   *

Silence is golden, but duct tape is silver

*   *   *   *

Little known fact:
Duck Tape is a brand of duct tape

*   *   *   *

Money doesn't buy happiness,
but I'd rather cry in my private jet

*   *   *   *

Avoid cliches like the plague

*   *   *   *

On this very site in 2011 nothing happened

*   *   *   *

Danger! Dinosaur area; keep out

*   *   *   *

Dead owls don't give a hoot

*   *   *   *

Small dogs are made of hard bark

*   *   *   *

I have seen the truth, and it makes no sense

*   *   *   *

Don't talk about yourself here;
we'll will do plenty of that when you leave

*   *   *   *

Come as strangers; leave as enemies

*   *   *   *

Few women admit their age; few men act theirs

*   *   *   *

Wow, it's nice out here in left field

*   *   *   *

My minions can take out your minions

*   *   *   *

Oops … did I just say that out loud?

*   *   *   *

I told my therapist about you!

*   *   *   *

Dr. Ahs on ATH

*   *   *   *

King of nothing in particular

*   *   *   *

Where are my peeps when I need them?

*   *   *   *

The voices in my head are slurring their words

*   *   *   *

Sorry! I can't hear you
over the sound of how suave I am

*   *   *   *

They're not deadlines, just guidelines

*   *   *   *

Deadlines amuse me

*   *   *   *

A goal is a dream with a deadline

*   *   *   *

12

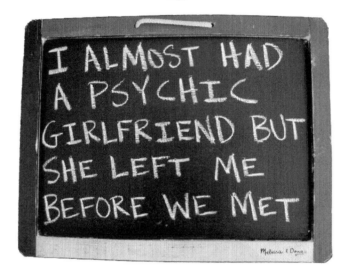

During a break in the show, I turned to Jason and said: "Did you see the eclipse of the moon last night? That was spectacular." He replied: "It was too dark." Guess what? *It was too dark to see the eclipse last night.*

*   *   *   *

The more you talk, the more my opinion matters

*   *   *   *

The city of happiness is in the state of mind

*   *   *   *

I was framed! –Chalk

*   *   *   *

If you want my attention pay me

*   *   *   *

If you can't speak, it's a mute point

*   *   *   *

I taught you everything I know,
and you still know nothing

*   *   *   *

I could describe apathy, but I'd rather not

*   *   *   *

Private sign: Please only look, don't read

*   *   *   *

I can't cook; I use a smoke alarm as a timer

*   *   *   *

Never eat anything you can't pronounce

*   *   *   *

You're so ugly you make onions cry

*   *   *   *

Show me your chalk

*   *   *   *

Peli can; chalkboard can't

*   *   *   *

Stop, drop and cinnamon roll!

*   *   *   *

All of my secrets are well known

*   *   *   *

About all I can make is a bag of chips open

*   *   *   *

I speak fluent sarcasm

*   *   *   *

Did you see the new pirate movie?
It's rated RRRRRgh

*   *   *   *

I can't believe I lost my watch;
I don't have time for this!

*   *   *   *

Every now and then,
I wish it was then instead of now

*   *   *   *

Procrastinators Unite! Tomorrow!

*   *   *   *

I'm lip-synching my answers today

*   *   *   *

I have a good knock knock joke; you start

*   *   *   *

I was going to draw a circle,
but there's just no point

*   *   *   *

If it weren't for people, there wouldn't be anybody

*   *   *   *

Keep it stupid simple

*   *   *   *

Why is the pizza box square,
when the pizza is round?

*   *   *   *

You can't mute the chalk!

*   *   *   *

If practice makes perfect and nobody's perfect,
why practice?

*   *   *   *

He who follows the beaten path seldom gets lost

*   *   *   *

Sometimes when I close my eyes, I can't see

*   *   *   *

If Monday had a face, I would punch it

*   *   *   *

The tree doesn't fall very far from the apple

*   *   *   *

3.14% of sailors are pi rates

*   *   *   *

I leave my mind at home so I don't lose it at work

*   *   *   *

Why did the chicken cross the playground?
To get to the other slide

*   *   *   *

< this space for rent >

*   *   *   *

Alright everybody,
line up alphabetically according to height

*   *   *   *

Object on screen may be smarter than he appears;
probably not, though

*   *   *   *

The best defence is a good spell-check

*   *   *   *

My Christmas list: chalk

*   *   *   *

Hi ho hi ho it's off to winning ATH I go,
but don't count on it, bro

*   *   *   *

I DVR ATH so I can mute Tony when I get home

*   *   *   *

In a game of lost and found, I lost

*   *   *   *

I write; therefore I'm right

*   *   *   *

I had an aquarium business, but it tanked

*   *   *   *

Hear about the circus fire? It was in tents

*   *   *   *

My envelope business failed because I mailed it in

*   *   *   *

My lamp is smart; it has a bright future

*   *   *   *

If 2 wrongs don't make a right, try 3!

*   *   *   *

When it rains and it's sunny,
I have mixed emotions

*   *   *   *

Kill the clock while you still have time

*   *   *   *

Who let the dogs out, wolff, wolff?
The dogs let themselves out, stupid

*   *   *   *

Can't was defeated in the battle of try

*   *   *   *

I'd say I'm happy to be here, but why lie?

*   *   *   *

Rectangles: Angles that text and drive

*   *   *   *

Celebrity astrology; it's all about the stars

*   *   *   *

This is a good bagel. Probably because it's a donut

*   *   *   *

I love my job. It's the work that I hate

*   *   *   *

I've got fingers on my blisters

*   *   *   *

What's the point of all this mute-iny?

*   *   *   *

Their. There. They're not the same

*   *   *   *

I'd make a terrible pessimist

*   *   *   *

Don't just do something, stand there

*   *   *   *

If winning was easy, losers would do it

*   *   *   *

Their are to meny badd spelers in the world

*   *   *   *

My chalk turns blue when I'm cold

*   *   *   *

My chalk turns red when I'm in love

*   *   *   *

My chalk turns green when I'm envious

*   *   *   *

I'd rather be seen than viewed

*   *   *   *

Laptops and projectors have nothing
on chalkboards

*   *   *   *

SARCASM:
Because arguing with these jokers is tedious

*   *   *   *

BEWARE: Facts and reasons
may appear without warning!

*   *   *   *

Sometimes I wish I were you ... so
I could be friends with me

*   *   *   *

I speak 3 different languages:
English, sports, and swearing

*   *   *   *

If time was on my side,
it would always be happy hour

*   *   *   *

You miss 100% of the shots you don't take

*   *   *   *

87% of short putts don't go in the cup

*   *   *   *

33% of the mutes on this show are the result of
Reali's hand slipping

*   *   *   *

Money may talk, but chocolate sings

*   *   *   *

Drama free zone

*   *   *   *

All the candy corn that was ever made
was made in 1912

*   *   *   *

I'd give up chocolate, but I'm no quitter

*   *   *   *

Eating fried pickles changed my life

*   *   *   *

I will attack you like a squirrel monkey

*   *   *   *

I like hanging out with my old ghoul friends

*   *   *   *

I am not arrogant. I'm just a lot better than you

*   *   *   *

A monkey could do my job, but I was here first

*   *   *   *

I'm not completely useless ...
I can be used as a bad example

*   *   *   *

Who cares if it's half-empty or half-full?
Just fill it up

*   *   *   *

Please wait ... I'm about to go sarcastic

*   *   *   *

King Kong went into beast mode

*   *   *   *

My genius is like lightning
One brilliant flash, and it's gone

*   *   *   *

My download has failed

*   *   *   *

Of course I'm right; I'm always right
I'm a truth machine

*   *   *   *

You laugh because I'm different
I laugh because you're all the same

*   *   *   *

Shhh … I'm in my happy place

*   *   *   *

Of course I don't look busy
I did it right the first time

*   *   *   *

Rosebud was my sled dog

*   *   *   *

Back by popular demand, not by choice

*   *   *   *

13

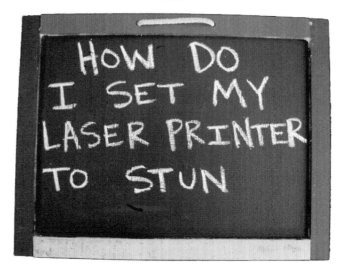

I like to do twists on movie lines and titles. Why? Because I do. Last year I had almost 600 chalkboard quotes behind me. Thus, some are not so sharp. Here's one from a popular movie of a few years ago; *No country for old men but ATH is for old me.*

*　　*　　*　　*

If you can't run with the big dogs,
get back on the porch

*　　*　　*　　*

If you're not the lead dog, the view never changes

*　　*　　*　　*

Every day I add a name to my hate list;
today's name is Henry The 8th

*   *   *   *

Leap year = 3 more buffets

*   *   *   *

Frogs love leap year

*   *   *   *

ATH: So easy a caveman could do it

*   *   *   *

Normal: Just a washing machine setting

*   *   *   *

I don't get mad; I get Mariotti

*   *   *   *

Career Goals: writer (checked), ninja (checked)

*   *   *   *

Picked last in P.E.

*   *   *   *

I'm serious, and don't call me Shirley

*   *   *   *

Oscar Madison nominee

*   *   *   *

There will be blood today

*   *   *   *

I am always right sometimes

*   *   *   *

If I wanted a friend I'd buy a dog

*   *   *   *

Charisma donor

*   *   *   *

Wherever I am, there's a party

*   *   *   *

This show works better if Tim doesn't talk

*   *   *   *

You're only young once,
but you're immature forever

*   *   *   *

Breakfast: raw egg, 2 aspirin, fresh mango,
cup of coffee

*   *   *   *

All I want is a little more than I'll ever get

*   *   *   *

I'm the person your parents warned you about!

*   *   *   *

I'm sick of being arm candy

*   *   *   *

Disgruntled employee of the month

*   *   *   *

Don't act stupid just because you know how to

*   *   *   *

Tan, rested and Helen Reddy

*   *   *   *

It's never too late to have a happy childhood!

*   *   *   *

I feel like the only tree in the kennel

*   *   *   *

It's been lovely but I have to scream now

*   *   *   *

Reboot the government

*   *   *   *

The government shut down;
how would we know?

*   *   *   *

It's not who you know, it's whom you know

*   *   *   *

I started with nothing; I still have most of it

*   *   *   *

Hard to make a comeback, Tony,
when you've been nowhere!

*   *   *   *

Bear takes over Disneyland in Pooh d'etat

*   *   *   *

I love the music

*   *   *   *

Hangin' with 3 fine clipboards

*   *   *   *

Cactus if you can

*   *   *   *

Life is too short, and so is Tony

*   *   *   *

I shout because Tony is hard of understanding

*   *   *   *

If the phone doesn't ring, Jay, you'll know it's me

*   *   *   *

Getting dumber just listening to you

*   *   *   *

Let's just disagree to agree with Cowlishaw

*   *   *   *

I eat paste

*   *   *   *

I'm just like Jackie, only louder & funnier

*   *   *   *

Tony doesn't want to read your blog

*   *   *   *

I see Mariott's point, but he's still wrong

*   *   *   *

Is today really necessary?

*   *   *   *

The more people I meet, the more I like my dog

*   *   *   *

Good kid gone bad

*   *   *   *

Warning! Will throw nearest object

*   *   *   *

Writer by day, superhero by night

*   *   *   *

In my world, there is no "I" in abbreviation

*   *   *   *

That's it, everyone gets a timeout

*   *   *   *

Rock is dead, long live paper & scissors

*   *   *   *

Always use spel cheker

*   *   *   *

Born to party, forced to work

*   *   *   *

Permanently on spin cycle

*   *   *   *

What's the abbreviation for abbreviation?

*   *   *   *

There's no life like low life; I should know

*   *   *   *

Smart is today, dumb is forever

*   *   *   *

Cooler than the other side of the pillow

*   *   *   *

I'm my own worst enemy; actually,
Mariotti is my worst enemy

*   *   *   *

Some do, some don't, I might

*   *   *   *

I talk to strangers

*   *   *   *

I see Jay's playing stupid, and he's winning

*   *   *   *

I make stuff up

*   *   *   *

I was big, I was easy, in the Big Easy

*   *   *   *

You can't sleep off ugly

*   *   *   *

Marriage: The leading cause of divorce

*   *   *   *

Clean-up on aisle Woody

*   *   *   *

None of the above

*   *   *   *

Mars is my home planet, and I want to go home,
but I can't get a ride

*   *   *   *

I took an I.Q. test, and the results were negative

*   *   *   *

My easy-going nature is being tested

*   *   *   *

Chocolate fixes everything

*   *   *   *

I'm so excited today, I'm scared

*   *   *   *

Plaschke's not getting bald, he's getting more brain

*   *   *   *

Bend it like Gumby

*   *   *   *

I'm currently being distracted by a shiny object

*   *   *   *

I'm right, you're wrong. Have a nice day

*   *   *   *

I used to think yelling was bad,
so I gave up thinking

*   *   *   *

I am one more loss away from owning 30 cats

*   *   *   *

Don't follow in my footsteps; I walk into walls

*   *   *   *

I plan on living forever; so far so good

*   *   *   *

Genius by birth, slacker by choice

*   *   *   *

My Loudness gives me superpowers

*   *   *   *

I have 2 speeds: loud and right

*   *   *   *

I feel diagonally parked in a parallel universe

*   *   *   *

I'm going to to CTL + ALT Delete Plaschke

*   *   *   *

Why do psychics ask your name?

*   *   *   *

Don't play leap frog with a unicorn

*   *   *   *

What's another word for thesaurus?

*   *   *   *

14

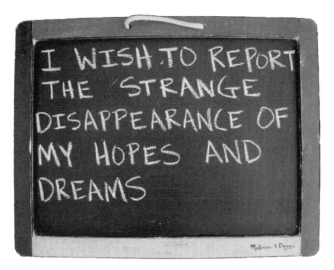

When I lived in Manhattan and did TV, I bought a book about where the TV and movie stars and famous athletes lived in the area. And on days when I wasn't working three shows from 3 a.m. until midnight, I would walk or drive to their homes. I saw Babe Ruth's and Woody Allen's apartments, and Joe DiMaggio's hotel suite, and John Lennon's place at the Dakota (where, outside, by Central Park, he was murdered).

But my favorite was the former home of Groucho Marx in Connecticut.

I idolized Groucho from his movies with his brothers, "A Night at the Opera" and "A Day at the Races," for instance, but I grew up watching him on the show "You Bet Your Life." He was hilarious with his snide and funny remarks and retorts, and I particularly liked the duck with the secret word. You have to watch it some time, and you can on Netflix and probably on a cable channel.

I stood outside Groucho's brick house and sprawling, wooded property and thought, 'What if he had a chalkboard behind him on TV?'

Talk about sayings:

"Alimony is like buying hay for a dead horse."

"I intend to live forever, or die trying."

"She got her face from her father. He was a plastic surgeon."

"I never forget a face, but I'll be glad to make an exception in your case."

"I would never belong to a club that would have me as a member."

And, "One morning I shot an elephant in my pajamas. How he got in my pajamas I'll never know."

When interviewed late in his life, Groucho said his epitaph on his grave would be, "Excuse me. I can't get up."

He was the master. Read the books about Groucho; watch his films and "You Bet Your Life."

Even though the following aren't in his class, these chalkboard sayings are for Groucho.

*   *   *   *

Who put a stop payment on my reality check?

*   *   *   *

You can tune a guitar, but you can't tuna fish

*   *   *   *

Worship me, and we'll get along just fine

*   *   *   *

Why does sour cream have an expiration date?

*   *   *   *

All life's answers are on this show

*   *   *   *

I'm a bottomless pit of needs and wants

*   *   *   *

My job is so secret—even I don't know what it is

*   *   *   *

I got street crud

*   *   *   *

I am a child of alien invaders

*   *   *   *

A pessimist is never disappointed

*   *   *   *

4 out of 5 voices in my head say "Go for it"

*   *   *   *

The next American Idle

*   *   *   *

I fix tires for a flat rate

*   *   *   *

A pediatrician is a doctor of little patience

*   *   *   *

Gasoline with carrot juice, you get beta mileage

*   *   *   *

When a clock is hungry it goes back four seconds

*   *   *   *

Mess with me,
and you mess with the whole trailer park

*   *   *   *

Laissez le bon temp rouler
("Let the good times roll")

*   *   *   *

For lunch I had a Mark Cuban sandwich

*   *   *   *

Successful dieters might win the nobelly prize

*   *   *   *

Nature reserves are an eagle opportunity employer

*   *   *   *

Cross-eyed teachers can't control their pupils

*   *   *   *

Reading while sunbathing makes you well-red

*   *   *   *

Some people don't like food going to waist

*   *   *   *

California smog test: can UCLA?

*   *   *   *

Flying these days is a frisky business

*   *   *   *

Small people are in short supply

*   *   *   *

Acupuncture is a jab well done

*   *   *   *

A criminal's best asset is his lie ability

*   *   *   *

A hangover is the wrath of grapes

*   *   *   *

What you seize is what you get

*   *   *   *

Two silk worms raced. They ended up in a tie

*   *   *   *

Those who hate classical music
have my symphony

*   *   *   *

Dermatologists often make rash statements

*   *   *   *

Pickle: Cucumber in trouble

*   *   *   *

Baldness is the cure for dandruff

*   *   *   *

Commentator: A talking spud

*   *   *   *

Artist: What the director of Around The Horn
thinks he is

*   *   *   *

Your ridiculous little opinion has been noted

*   *   *   *

The young know the rules;
the old know the exceptions

*   *   *   *

Sumo wrestling is survival of the fattest

*   *   *   *

I am vary disappointment in you're grammar

*   *   *   *

Don't act like you're not impressed

*   *   *   *

I have not yet begun to procrastinate

*   *   *   *

Not only am I perfect, I'm Irish, too!

*   *   *   *

Who's your paddy?

*   *   *   *

Better to understand a little
than to misunderstand a lot

*   *   *   *

"I have a split personality", said Tony,
being Frank today

*   *   *   *

Are the voices in my head
keeping you up at night?

*   *   *   *

Debate: Babble instead of battle

*　　　*　　　*　　　*

Beethoven was so deaf
he thought he was a painter

*　　　*　　　*　　　*

Nylons give women a run for their money

*　　　*　　　*　　　*

Country music is three chords and the truth

*　　　*　　　*　　　*

Mermaid: A deep she fish

*　　　*　　　*　　　*

Relish today. Ketchup tomorrow

*　　　*　　　*　　　*

My other car is a UFO

*　　　*　　　*　　　*

Thesaurus: A dinosaur with a big vocabulary

*　　　*　　　*　　　*

I'm heavily medicated for your safety

*　　　*　　　*　　　*

If you want breakfast in bed in my house,
sleep in the kitchen

*　　　*　　　*　　　*

Frankly, scallop, I don't give a clam

*　　　*　　　*　　　*

Don't talk unless you can improve the silence

*　　　*　　　*　　　*

Academy Awards: A place where
everyone lets off esteem

*   *   *   *

Hollywood Marriage: Much "I do" about nothing

*   *   *   *

ESP-N: A new cable channel
for psychics who like sports

*   *   *   *

I used to be indecisive, but I'm not sure now

*   *   *   *

Fine print: A clause for suspicion

*   *   *   *

The best things in life are duty-free

*   *   *   *

Today's subliminal message is:

*   *   *   *

Reali: Support your local search and rescue—
get lost!

*   *   *   *

Stop illitrissy now!

*   *   *   *

I am not a pessimist, but my future looks bleak

*   *   *   *

I am logged in, therefore I am

*   *   *   *

Hire a teenager now—while
he still knows everything

*   *   *   *

Give blood—play hockey

*   *   *   *

Due to lack of interest, today has been postponed;
tomorrow is uncertain

*   *   *   *

I was my school's spelling bee champ
in fifth grade. (Realy)

*   *   *   *

I think, therefore I am overqualified

*   *   *   *

I'm not paranoid. There are 150,000 following
me … on twitter. They're out to get me

*   *   *   *

Don't you just hate rhetorical questions?

*   *   *   *

My secret on ATH is that, like in the Lassie
movies, there are four blackboards
Each can do different tricks

*   *   *   *

Don't rush me,
I'm making mistakes as fast as I can

*   *   *   *

I'm making this up as I go along

*   *   *   *

It's gonna be like threading a needle
with a haystack

*   *   *   *

No electrons were harmed
in the creation of this message

*   *   *   *

No animals were harmed
in the taping of this show

*   *   *   *

The facts, though interesting, are irrelevant

*   *   *   *

I don't get even, I get odder

*   *   *   *

Math problems? Call 0800-[(12x)(-y3)]-xy2.3

*   *   *   *

Before ESPN was invented,
what was the purpose of a sports bar?

*   *   *   *

Me a skeptic? I hope you have proof

*   *   *   *

Before they invented drawing boards,
what did they go back to?

*   *   *   *

Before they invented blackboards,
where did they write sayings?

*   *   *   *

Do pediatricians play miniature golf
on Wednesday?

*   *   *   *

Bald Eagle: Large bird too vain to buy a hairpiece

* * * *

Men are from Earth. Women are from Earth.
Deal with it

* * * *

Driveway: where you park; Parkway:
Where you drive

* * * *

Loved by FEW, Hated by MANY, Feared by ALL

* * * *

Why are they called apartments
when they're all stuck together?

* * * *

Why are they called buildings
when they're already built?

* * * *

Why is the place at the airport
where you go to get on a plane called "terminal"?

* * * *

I just got lost in thought.
It was unfamiliar territory

* * * *

I'm planning to be more spontaneous
in the future

* * * *

If you try to fail, and succeed,
which have you done?

* * * *

I have a mind like a steel trap,
rusty and illegal in 39 states

*   *   *   *

A conclusion is the place
where you got tired of thinking

*   *   *   *

I can explain it to you,
but I can't understand it for you

*   *   *   *

Sometimes when I'm alone, I Google myself

*   *   *   *

Whenever I feel blue, I start breathing again

*   *   *   *

Banging your head against a wall
uses up 150 calories (per hr)

*   *   *   *

The electric chair was invented by a dentist

*   *   *   *

No President of the United States
was an only child

*   *   *   *

If you can read this, you're too close to the page

*   *   *   *

15

Jason and I were talking before the show about the origin of the term 'around the horn.' I told him the baseball term was based on the infielders throwing the ball to each other, after an out, around the infield, or, around the horn. A 5-4-3 double play (third baseman to second baseman to first baseman) also could be considered around the horn.

'Around the horn' is actually an old sailing idiom. Before the Panama Canal was cut through Central America, ships traveling from the Atlantic to the Pacific would have to sail to the bottom of South America and go 'around the horn;' Cape Horn, which was located at the tip of Chile.

Baseball also utilizes a couple of other ship phrases. The next batter is 'on deck' and the following batter is 'in the hold,' although that idiom has been altered over the years to 'in the hole.'

Jason and I decided to offer chalkboard sayings based on 'around the horn.' Like some of these ones. See if you can guess which!

*   *   *   *

To err is human, to arr is pirate

*   *   *   *

National Talk like a Pirate day

*   *   *   *

Blackbeard had a blackberry

*   *   *   *

Buoy or sails

*   *   *   *

Johnny Depp's Grandfather

*   *   *   *

Pirates love to cheer for the Toronto Arrrgonauts

*   *   *   *

Did the constant gardener play around the thorns?

*   *   *   *

Whenever I go near a bank
I get withdrawal symptoms

*   *   *   *

The difference between a champ
and a chump is U

*   *   *   *

Meantime: hate o'clock

*   *   *   *

A calculator is a product you can count on!

*   *   *   *

I am built for sloppy, not speed

*   *   *   *

My calendar days are numbered

*   *   *   *

Faster than the speed of mute

*   *   *   *

Blackboard chalks in its sleep

*   *   *   *

Please explain the scoring system one more time,
Tony, since none of us understand

*   *   *   *

Accountants can count on me!

*   *   *   *

I don't care about apathetic people

*   *   *   *

I'll start listening when Cowlishaw stops talking

*   *   *   *

Authors always write me off

*   *   *   *

I don't write incomplete sentences since the

*   *   *   *

My stunts were confirmed on Mythbusters

*   *   *   *

My 3 favorite months are Septober,
Octember, and Decober

*   *   *   *

What do hobbyists do for fun?

*   *   *   *

I demand my 10% senior point allowance

*   *   *   *

Reali should score on the curve

*   *   *   *

A corndog is a hotdog wearing a sweater

*   *   *   *

If I am here to help others,
what exactly are the others here for?

*   *   *   *

I'm an ice sculptor. Last night I carved a cube

*   *   *   *

I'm against picketing;
I just don't know how to show it

*   *   *   *

Unicorns are real; a leprechaun told me so

*   *   *   *

Everyone has a right to be stupid.
I just abuse the privilege

*   *   *   *

I am not repetitive or redundant

*   *   *   *

I think the freezer deserves a light, too

*   *   *   *

Anything that is unrelated to elephants
is irrelephant

*   *   *   *

I'm not sure, but I think I don't know

*   *   *   *

The truth is out there somewhere
So what are you doing here?

*   *   *   *

How do people with multiple personalities
fill out their census papers?

*   *   *   *

A toast to bread, for without bread,
there would be no toast

*   *   *   *

Now accepting coupons and compliments

*   *   *   *

My mind is closed this week for repairs

*   *   *   *

If silence is a weapon, then I am defenseless!

*   *   *   *

Do catfish have nine lives?

*   *   *   *

I don't live in fantasy; I only work there

*   *   *   *

Young at heart, slightly older in other places

*   *   *   *

Life takes its toll. Bring change

*   *   *   *

When all is said and done, more is said than done

*   *   *   *

How did the "Keep off the grass" signs get there?

*   *   *   *

I was on a roll, until I slipped on the butter

*   *   *   *

It should be written in concrete:
Keep off the cement

*   *   *   *

Keep out, or you will be let in

*   *   *   *

Sign in ATH control room:
Producers must wash hands after every show

*   *   *   *

Trespassers will be hugged

*   *   *   *

Beware of good dog

*   *   *   *

Please leave on your shoes

*   *   *   *

It's lonely at the top, but you eat better

*   *   *   *

Do not read this sign

*   *   *   *

You get what you settle for

*   *   *   *

You can't steal second with your foot on first

*   *   *   *

Either I get what I want or I change my mind

*   *   *   *

This space left intentionally blank

*   *   *   *

You can't fall off the floor

*   *   *   *

Last night I broke my hand when leaving the bar
because someone stepped on it

*   *   *   *

Every show is the dawn of a new error

*   *   *   *

Now is not a good time to annoy me

*   *   *   *

My mom thinks I'm at the library
every day during ATH

*   *   *   *

Sit back and enjoy the chaos

*   *   *   *

A well done medium is rare

*   *   *   *

The Internet is now closed. Please log off

*   *   *   *

I fought Chuck Norris, and it was pretty much a
draw unless you count the blood on my face
and my broken bones

*   *   *   *

I'd win almost every day if I was the only panelist

*   *   *   *

I should have worn a helmet in Little League
baseball and dodgeball

*   *   *   *

I might flip, but I won't flop

*   *   *   *

I don't use lead-based chalk!

*   *   *   *

Donuts are great bracelets to wear
if you're in the desert for a month

*   *   *   *

ATH scoring is as legit as WWE

*   *   *   *

Blackboard is a free agent and available
to highest-bidding TV game show,
especially "The Price Is Right"

*   *   *   *

My best friends are imaginary

*   *   *   *

I've tested positive for GummiBears

*   *   *   *

My get up and go got up and went

* * * *

I can't even afford a Po' Boy sandwich

* * * *

I'm on a hunger strike in between meals

* * * *

I wasn't late today; I was early for tomorrow

* * * *

Yelling is the only exercise I get

* * * *

I've tried all the early-bird specials

* * * *

I'll bet you a dollar you'll read this

* * * *

I want to supply my own questions

* * * *

Last night I dreamed I had insomnia

* * * *

When alone, I'm the smartest person in the room

* * * *

5 out of 4 dentists recommend ATH

* * * *

The mute button violates the first amendment

* * * *

Talk is cheap; chalk is cheaper

* * * *

The rabbit lost to the tortoise by a hare

*   *   *   *

What happened to Humpty Dumpty
was not an accident

*   *   *   *

Chicken Little was the victim of fowl play

*   *   *   *

Tony mutes due to a lack of social graces

*   *   *   *

The mute is the highest form of disrespect

*   *   *   *

10,339 career mutes and counting

*   *   *   *

The muting will continue until morale improves

*   *   *   *

Mute if you love me

*   *   *   *

Panic now, and avoid the rush

*   *   *   *

16

A waitress at Bubba Gump (yes, I have my own table there) came up and said, "I have a $2 bet with the manager that you're Woody Paige."

"Do I get half if you win?"

Usually, when people ask if I'm "that guy with the blackboard" (which happens about 30 times a day), I reply, "Depends if I owe you money."

The manager approaches and says: "I have a saying for you. Will you use it?"

"Only if it's good."

And she says, "Practice safe lunch, use a condiment."

Jason and I looked at each other. Well, Jason looked at me; I was watching his skin turn the color of ketchup. "OK," I said. "I'll put it on the chalkboard Friday."

I still want that dollar, though. Shrimp is expensive.

*   *   *   *

In an airport on one trip, I bought this new flavor of potato chips; Ketchup potato chips. Yuck. You don't put ketchup on potato chips. But it gave me a blackboard; *I put ketchup on my ketchup.*

*   *   *   *

If you are what you eat, I'm fast, cheap, & easy

*   *   *   *

What if the hokey pokey really is
what it's all about?

*   *   *   *

Chaos, panic, and disorder. My work here is done

*   *   *   *

I have a protective covering for my rock hard abs

*   *   *   *

Excess is never too much in moderation

*   *   *   *

You had me at mute

*   *   *   *

All I ask is that you treat me no differently
than a king

*   *   *   *

Don't try this at home; I'm an amateur

*   *   *   *

If at first you don't succeed,
skydiving is not for you

*   *   *   *

Money is the root of all evil
Send me $10 for more information

*   *   *   *

I love me some me

*   *   *   *

Blame Captain Kangaroo for the way I am

*   *   *   *

I know everything, just not all at once

*   *   *   *

People who think they know it all
really annoy those of us who do

*   *   *   *

I'm schizophrenic, and so am I

*   *   *   *

Stable relationships are for horses

*   *   *   *

I want more Mariotti Marriott points

*   *   *   *

It's a Favre Favre better thing Brett did

*   *   *   *

For my next trick
I need Plaschke & a mute button

*   *   *   *

I'm the Lying King, and
Dikembe Mutombo means no worries

*   *   *   *

Without geometry, math has no point

*   *   *   *

On your mark, get set, go away!

*   *   *   *

If it weren't for the gutter
my mind would be homeless

*   *   *   *

Life's a garden. Can you dig it?

*   *   *   *

Of all the things I've lost, I miss my mind most

*   *   *   *

Hugs are better than drugs

*   *   *   *

Take the L out of lover. We are over

*   *   *   *

You only live once (maybe)

*   *   *   *

A closed mouth gathers no feet

*   *   *   *

Proofreading are for lazy persons

*   *   *   *

Instant swimmer. Just add water

*   *   *   *

Clothes required, underwear optional

*   *   *   *

Leave me alone. I'm having a crisis

*   *   *   *

Why are you reading this?

*   *   *   *

My karma ran over your dogma

*   *   *   *

Ask me. I might

*   *   *   *

Even the simplest job can be done rong

*   *   *   *

I'm so adjective I verb nouns

*   *   *   *

If at first you don't succeed, call it version 1.0

*   *   *   *

You're just jealous because the voices
only talk to me

*   *   *   *

Vegetarian: Armenian word for lousy hunter

*   *   *   *

Rap is to music as Etch-A-Sketch is to art

*   *   *   *

The trouble with the gene pool is
that there's no lifeguard

*   *   *   *

My mother is a travel agent for guilt trips

*   *   *   *

There's a time & place for everything
It's called Around The Horn

*   *   *   *

I'm trying to imagine you
with a personality Mariotti!

*   *   *   *

Whatever kind of look you were going for,
you missed the mark

*   *   *   *

Well, this day was a total waste of makeup

*   *   *   *

Change is inevitable
except from vending machines

*   *   *   *

Every time I get it together I forget where I put it

*   *   *   *

I am not infantile, you stinky poopyhead

*   *   *   *

After four karate lessons,
I can now break a board with my cast

*   *   *   *

I walk everywhere for my health but I never find it

* * * *

When in doubt, mumble; when in trouble,
delegate; when in charge, ponder

* * * *

Diamonds are forever, Mr. Bond;
the payments take longer

* * * *

The way I keep looking young
is by hanging out with old people

* * * *

I don't have an attitude;
I have a personality you can't handle

* * * *

It matters not whether you win or lose;
it matters whether or not I win or lose

* * * *

We'll all get along fine as soon as
you realize I'm right all the time

* * * *

I've never understood decimals.
I can't see the point in them

* * * *

The difference between genius and stupidity is
that genius has its limits

* * * *

I'm objective; I object to everything

* * * *

The ultimate reason, my mom told me,
is "because"

*   *   *   *

It's not what you say in your argument,
it's how loud you say it

*   *   *   *

If you can't learn to do it well,
learn to enjoy doing it badly

*   *   *   *

Abandon the search for truth;
settle for a good fantasy

*   *   *   *

I cannot achieve the impossible
without attempting the absurd

*   *   *   *

No matter where you go, you're almost there

*   *   *   *

Your lucky color has faded

*   *   *   *

My rules apply only to other people

*   *   *   *

Adults are just kids with money

*   *   *   *

Why should I grow up? I agree with Peter Pan
This is more fun!

*   *   *   *

Life without bears would be unbearable

*   *   *   *

Life is tough; get a helmet

*   *   *   *

No shirt no shoes bad service

*   *   *   *

Two wrongs don't make a right, but three lefts do

*   *   *   *

Whoever said nothing is impossible
never tried slamming a revolving door

*   *   *   *

I installed my DVR myself.
Now I get movies on my vacuum cleaner

*   *   *   *

I asked my assistant to take a letter
He picked "R"

*   *   *   *

Don't let your mind wander
It's too small to be let out alone

*   *   *   *

He's really tough.
He went to reform school on scholarship

*   *   *   *

I don't lie, cheat or steal—unnecessarily

*   *   *   *

Since I gave up hope, I feel much better

*   *   *   *

Don't listen to me; I am confused

*   *   *   *

In my family tree, I'm the sap

*   *   *   *

Never get in a spitting contest with a llama

*   *   *   *

I can handle pain until it hurts

*   *   *   *

If money can't buy happiness,
I guess you'll just have to rent it

*   *   *   *

Everything I need to know
I learned from Gilligan's Island

*   *   *   *

I loved Lovey more than Ginger and Mary Ann

*   *   *   *

I'm more like the Professor than the Skipper

*   *   *   *

17

We bought a new glass-topped table for our studio (which is about the size of a small bedroom) and my associate Jason decided he could assemble it. Two days later we had a table for my research packet and the Diet Coke (with peanuts in the bottle—a southern tradition) I drink every day. Just as we were to begin taping a segment for the show, I stood up to shut the door.

And the glass instantaneously shattered all over the room. Not the floor. The room. Really.

Jason and I stare at each other. Both of us are covered in glass, but we're not injured or bleeding.

"We coulda died," Jason said.

"Nice job of putting the table together," I said.

"Not my fault," he said.

"I think the glass was screwed on a little too tight. So, if it's not your fault, it's an Act of God."

"He doesn't want you to be on TV."

"What a revolting development."

I sat down and did the show with glass all over the room and my clothes, and this was the first chalkboard quote of the day: *Beware of glass tables that explode; somebody may be trying to tell you something.*

*   *   *   *

Shoddy workmanship is not a promise;
it's a guarantee

*   *   *   *

Mona Lisa has no eyebrows

*   *   *   *

Tact is for people who aren't witty

*   *   *   *

Clothing optional beyond this point

*   *   *   *

$35 charge for listening to your whining

*   *   *   *

A cockroach can live up to 10 days with no head

*   *   *   *

The Hundred Years War actually lasted 116 years

*   *   *   *

Penguins can jump up to 6 feet, but who cares?

*   *   *   *

I have a reputation to live down

*   *   *   *

It sure makes the day longer
when I get to work on time

*   *   *   *

I love hyperbole the most

*   *   *   *

I am cleverly disguised as a responsible adult

*   *   *   *

I only make sense in closed captioning

*   *   *   *

I'm in a place where I don't know where I am

*   *   *   *

My train of thought has been delayed
at the station

*   *   *   *

I'm currently being distracted because of a full
stomach and a full moon

*   *   *   *

What happens if you're scared
half to death TWICE?

*   *   *   *

I would thank you for caring, but I don't care

*   *   *   *

Can your inner child come out and play?

*   *   *   *

La la la I can't hear you

*   *   *   *

When I die,
I want to come back as Beaver Cleaver

*   *   *   *

I came to chew gum & win ATH
I'm all out of gum

*   *   *   *

Someday we'll look back on this, laugh nervously
and quickly change the subject

*   *   *   *

If it fits in a toaster, I can cook it

*   *   *   *

I am still hot. It just comes in flashes

*   *   *   *

Kurt Vonnegut said to never use semi-colons in
writing; he was certainly correct

*   *   *   *

Never go to a doctor
whose office plants have died

*   *   *   *

Watching me online is virtually the best

*   *   *   *

I'm part genius, part buffoon

*   *   *   *

A bird in hand is safer than one overhead

*   *   *   *

Strangely enough, only 26% of pirates wear
prescription eye patches

*   *   *   *

Everyone says I'm in denial, but I'm not

*   *   *   *

John told me a house without a toilet is uncanny

*   *   *   *

Men who sit on tacks get the point
Do you get my point?

*   *   *   *

Those who live in glass houses
should change in the basement

*   *   *   *

Help! I've fallen, and I can't shut up

*   *   *   *

Known best for our customer service:
Putting people on hold since 1959

*   *   *   *

I'll make this sound cooler in my blog
and my memoirs

*   *   *   *

Men who run behind cars get exhausted

*   *   *   *

I use Jedi mind tricks
when I'm in the Showdown portion of the show

*   *   *   *

Sorry, but I'm ridiculously good,
and I've never been known to exaggerate

*   *   *   *

Don't argue. I've been sautéed in right sauce

*   *   *   *

Send in the chimp; I'm taking
the rest of the day off to monkey around

*   *   *   *

Save the drama for yo' mama

*   *   *   *

A jellyfish is 95% water

*   *   *   *

Clinophobia is the fear of beds

*   *   *   *

Porcupines float in water

*   *   *   *

You can't be considered late until you show up!

*   *   *   *

Free advice is worth what you paid for it

*   *   *   *

Dollar bills no longer are worth
the paper they're printed on

*   *   *   *

It's good to be clever, but not to show it

*   *   *   *

Sometimes I feel like a nut, sometimes I don't,
then I feel like a cashew

* * * *

I don't play with a broken finger; Pinky Lee would

* * * *

Better a witty fool than a foolish wit

* * * *

I have an inferiority complex,
but it's not a good one

* * * *

The average person thinks he isn't

* * * *

Misfortunes and twins never come singly

* * * *

Happiness is good health and a bad memory

* * * *

Listening to Tim is like wading through glue

* * * *

Déjà Moo:
The feeling that you have met this cow before

* * * *

Mecca lecca hi, mecca hiney ho

* * * *

I have a keen sense of rumor

* * * *

It's wrong to ever split an infinitive

* * * *

Some mistakes are to much fun
too make just once

*   *   *   *

At my age, the happy hour is a nap

*   *   *   *

Touche, twoche

*   *   *   *

Avoid parking tickets
by leaving your wipers turned on high

*   *   *   *

To write with a broken pencil is pointless

*   *   *   *

The older I get, the better I was

*   *   *   *

Who copyrighted the copyright system?

*   *   *   *

Does the name Pavlov ring a bell?

*   *   *   *

In case of emergency, speak in clichés

*   *   *   *

Poets have been curiously silent about cheese

*   *   *   *

If you put "the" and "IRS" together,
it spells "theirs"

*   *   *   *

Bad breath is better than no breath at all

*   *   *   *

My main purpose in life
is to serve as a warning to others

*   *   *   *

I know an archeologist whose career,
sadly, is in ruins

*   *   *   *

Yawn: An honest reaction, openly expressed

*   *   *   *

Thanksgiving: Not a good day to be my stomach

*   *   *   *

What do I look like? Flypaper for freaks?

*   *   *   *

When do you want to meet? How about never?
Is never good for you?

*   *   *   *

I don't work here. I'm a consultant

*   *   *   *

Also, too, never, ever use repetitive redundancies

*   *   *   *

And don't start a sentence with a conjunction

*   *   *   *

I'm not the best panelist, but I'm in the top 1%

*   *   *   *

Am I ambivalent? Yes and no

*   *   *   *

False hope is nicer than no hope at all

*   *   *   *

Broken guitar for sale. No strings attached

*   *   *   *

Being young is a flaw that diminishes daily

*   *   *   *

In a bar, is it fall forward and spring back?

*   *   *   *

I have a stomach virus. "Alimentary"
says Sherlock Holmes

*   *   *   *

18

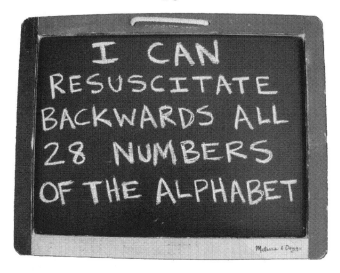

One night I was watching a baseball game, and a car commercial interrupted. "GOOD CREDIT, NO PROBLEM," the automobile dealer shouted. "BAD CREDIT, NO PROBLEM. NO CREDIT, *NO PROBLEM!*" I thought, 'Sure.'

So when I went into the studio the next day I told Jason I wanted these two blackboard sayings:

Good credit, no problem. Bad credit, no problem. No credit, problem.

My credit is so bad they won't even take my cash.

*   *   *   *

Nursery rhymes confuse me

*   *   *   *

I do my daily exercises weekly

*   *   *   *

When I want your opinion, I'll give it to you

*   *   *   *

If you're looking for me,
I just left right before you got here

*   *   *   *

I know you are, but who am I to say?

*   *   *   *

Just say no to innuendo

*   *   *   *

Don't look at me in that tone of voice

*   *   *   *

The weather is here. Wish you were beautiful

*   *   *   *

I'm enjoying my vacation. Wish you were her

*   *   *   *

I don't know, I don't care,
and it doesn't matter, anyway

*   *   *   *

Werewolves are real; Dracula told me so

*   *   *   *

Can I use my double points coupons today?

*   *   *   *

I was behind when I showed up

*   *   *   *

Always open: closed until further notice

*   *   *   *

I never ever speak in absolutes

*   *   *   *

Magic is a vanishing art

*   *   *   *

Old magicians never die. They just disappear

*   *   *   *

Lefties have rights, too

*   *   *   *

I shop like a bull. I charge everything

*   *   *   *

Can I pay off my VISA with my library card?

*   *   *   *

Don't laugh. Someday I'll
be in charge of the world

*   *   *   *

My only domestic quality is that I live in a house

*   *   *   *

If you can read this, thank your teacher

*   *   *   *

It's as bad as you think and they are out to get you

*   *   *   *

I'm paid weekly. Very weakly

*   *   *   *

Money is the root of all evil. I'm OK with evil

*   *   *   *

I'm so broke I can't even pay attention

*   *   *   *

Mother said there would be days like this, but she
didn't say there would be an entire decade like this

*   *   *   *

Eat 1 live toad first thing in the morning,
and nothing bad will happen
to you for the rest of the day

*   *   *   *

How come "slow down" and "slow up"
mean the same thing?

*   *   *   *

I used to be a proofreader
for a skywriting company

*   *   *   *

I have a map of the U.S. that's life-sized:
1 mile = 1 mile

*   *   *   *

I have a large seashell collection,
which I have placed on beaches all over the world

*   *   *   *

When I put my ear to a conch shell, I hear ATH

*   *   *   *

The fact that no one understands you
doesn't mean you're an artist

* * * *

Money doesn't talk; it goes without saying

* * * *

If stupidity was music, I'd be a one-man band

* * * *

That's a nice suit Tony. Who shines it for you?

* * * *

Don't bother me. I'm living happily ever after

* * * *

98% of the time I'm right
Why worry about the other half?

* * * *

National Sarcasm Society:
Like we need your support

* * * *

Now using HD-chalk

* * * *

A synonym is a word you use
when you can't spell the other one

* * * *

Living on Earth may be expensive but it includes
an annual free trip around the sun

* * * *

An apple a day keeps the doctor away,
but an onion keeps everyone away

*   *   *   *

The less we know, the longer the explanation

*   *   *   *

Cowlishaw is just doing a Weird Al parody of me

*   *   *   *

If the sky is the limit, then what is space?

*   *   *   *

Being muted is time well spent

*   *   *   *

Me doing ATH is found money

*   *   *   *

Why are there 5 syllables in monosyllabic?

*   *   *   *

I'm not afraid of work;
you can tell by the way I fight it

*   *   *   *

Cynics claim they are right eleven out of ten times

*   *   *   *

A lawyer writes a 10,000-word document
and calls it a brief

*   *   *   *

Professor Blackistone talks in someone else's sleep

*   *   *   *

Stat Boy: A person who is good with numbers,
but lacks personality

*   *   *   *

Accountant: Someone who knows the cost of
everything and the value of nothing

*   *   *   *

Consultant: A person who takes your watch
and tells you the time

*   *   *   *

My opinions have changed,
but not the fact that I'm right

*   *   *   *

No matter what goes wrong,
there's always someone who knew it would

*   *   *   *

Beware the fury of the patient panelist

*   *   *   *

Never invest in anything
that eats or needs repairing

*   *   *   *

Things equal to nothing else
are equal to each other

*   *   *   *

If at first you don't succeed, QUIT!

*   *   *   *

If at first you don't succeed, try management

*   *   *   *

If at first you don't succeed, get a job on this show

*   *   *   *

To err is human. To admit it isn't

*   *   *   *

You're stressed when you can hear mimes

*   *   *   *

Why isn't there mouse-flavored cat food?

*   *   *   *

Some drink at the fountain of knowledge
I just gargle

*   *   *   *

Why is an actor IN a movie, but ON television?

*   *   *   *

What disease did cured ham have?

*   *   *   *

Discretion is being able to raise your eyebrow
instead of your voice

*   *   *   *

Do Roman paramedics refer to IVs as "4s"?

*   *   *   *

I wondered why the baseball kept getting bigger
Then it hit me

*   *   *   *

The shortest distance between two points
is always under construction

*   *   *   *

Never do card tricks for your poker buddies

*   *   *   *

Tony and I always compromise.
I admit I'm wrong, and he agrees with me

*   *   *   *

Tony keeps complaining that I never listen to
him ... or something like that

*   *   *   *

Tony is someone who always sees
the bright side of your problem

*   *   *   *

Trust me, but always ask for my driver's license

*   *   *   *

To err is human, to blame it on Tony
shows managerial potential

*   *   *   *

With sufficient thrust, pigs indeed fly just fine

*   *   *   *

Worrying works. 90% of the things I worry about
never happen

*   *   *   *

You're never too old to learn something stupid

*   *   *   *

A sharp tongue does not mean
you have a keen mind

*   *   *   *

How do I draw a blank?

*   *   *   *

I'm validating my inherent distrust of strangers

*   *   *   *

What would Scooby Doo?

*   *   *   *

How come we say "tunafish" but not
"beefmammal" or "chickenbird"?

*   *   *   *

It's easier to get older than to get wiser

*   *   *   *

Thank you Tony! We're all refreshed and
challenged by your unique point of view

*   *   *   *

I'm busy. Can I ignore you another time?

*   *   *   *

I finally got my head together,
and now my body is falling apart

*   *   *   *

How can there be self-help groups?

*   *   *   *

Bill sounds reasonable today.
I think it's time to increase my medication

*   *   *   *

When I'm finally holding all the cards,
why does everyone else decide to play chess?

*   *   *   *

Thousands have lived without love,
not one without ATH

*   *   *   *

Who am I calling stupid? Good question
What's your name?

*   *   *   *

Money can't buy everything, but then again,
neither can no money

*   *   *   *

I'm moving to Mars next week,
so if you have any boxes …

*   *   *   *

My watch is 2 hours fast, and I can't fix it,
so I'm moving back to New York

*   *   *   *

I bought some powdered water
but don't know what to add

*   *   *   *

I talk to myself a lot, and it bothers other people
because I use a megaphone

*   *   *   *

I like to leave messages before the beep

*   *   *   *

O.S.H.A. mandate: Recall all mute buttons

*   *   *   *

Sometimes I don't even understand me

*   *   *   *

19

In 1955, a 9 year-old boy was mesmerized by a new, daily afternoon show on TV. "The Mickey Mouse Club" made its debut with Jimmie Dodd (a song and dance man) as the host, and a group of boys and girls as the Mouseketeers.

Several cast members came to Memphis to promote the show's start, and I persuaded my mom to take me on the bus to the theater downtown to meet them and get some autographs. Even at 9, I was in love, as was every other boy of that generation, with Annette Funicello, but Spin of "Spin and Marty," a regular serial on the show, was the kid I really liked. Mostly, I wanted to be a Mouseketeer.

Alas, that wasn't going to happen. But I also wanted to be the batboy of the Giants or the Yankees. The batboys of those two teams wrote their own biographies, and I read them over and over again every summer with my other favorite book, "The Year the Yankees Lost the Pennant," which became the Broadway play, "Damn Yankees."

There was also a brief time when I wanted to grow up to be Davy Crockett.

Strange, but many years later, I would work for the same parent company as Annette, Cubby, Darlene and Bobby, and in some ways I became Spin to another guy's Marty. We did a bunch of shows from Disney World, and boys and girls told me they wanted to grow up and be like me. What a disgusting thought if the world was filled with people like me.

My saying to students at Tennessee last year when I got a Distinguised Alumni award was, "If the worst, incorrigible student ever at Tennessee can make it in the world, imagine what you, as good, intelligent students, can accomplish."

"Get yourself a blackboard."

*   *   *   *

Jealousy is a disease. Get well soon, Jay

*   *   *   *

Aliens are abducting sexy old people. I just wanted
to say goodbye

*   *   *   *

Men who eat crackers in bed
wake up feeling crummy

*   *   *   *

Yoga is for posers

*   *   *   *

Math uses: 50% equations; 50% proofs;
50% formulas

*   *   *   *

Camels have 3 eyelids; slugs have 4 noses;
I have 1/2 a brain. Please explain

*   *   *   *

A line is a dot that went for a walk

*   *   *   *

OK, so what's the speed of dark?

*   *   *   *

I'm a Vol-in-tears

*   *   *   *

Come to the dork side

*   *   *   *

ATH is a circus, and I'm in the freak tent

*   *   *   *

Man with 1 chopstick go hungry

*   *   *   *

I'm Woody Paige, and
I don't approve of this message

*   *   *   *

I can predict yesterday's scores

*   *   *   *

Never play strip ATH with Plaschke

*   *   *   *

Please don't sue me when I blow your mind
with my answers

*   *   *   *

UFOs are real. Bigfoot told me so

*   *   *   *

Cows are just too mooooody;
former pro golfer Orville Moody also was

*   *   *   *

Most lies about me are completely false

*   *   *   *

I don't mispronounciate my words

*   *   *   *

I'm a dealer in high-grade fertilizer

*   *   *   *

If life is a stage, I'd like better lighting

*   *   *   *

Please do not feed or tease the fantasy geeks

*   *   *   *

Parsley has as much importance on a plate as
Cowlishaw does on this show

*   *   *   *

Frog parking ←→ All others toad

*   *   *   *

What do sign makers hold when they go on strike?

*   *   *   *

What do little birdies see
when they get knocked out?

*   *   *   *

I think I may stop being indecisive; perhaps not

*   *   *   *

If a cow laughs hard, does milk come out its nose?

*   *   *   *

If the #2 pencil is the best, why is it still #2?

*   *   *   *

Why does fat chance = slim chance?

*   *   *   *

I poured Spot Remover on my dog,
and now I can't find him

*   *   *   *

My French teacher was muy caliente!

*   *   *   *

I hear voices, and they don't like you

*   *   *   *

Be careful playing Scrabble; it can be dangerous;
you could lose an i

*   *   *   *

Bad listeners are ear responsible

*   *   *   *

Don't forget these 3 things ... I forget

*   *   *   *

Scars are tattoos with better stories

*   *   *   *

I've thought about running about more
as an adult than I did as a child

*   *   *   *

I'm right most of the time;
I'm delusional for the rest of it

*   *   *   *

You mean to tell me this is only 2 percent milk—
what's the rest of it?

*   *   *   *

I like cooking with wine;
sometimes I even put it in the food

*   *   *   *

I call my bathroom Jim;
it sounds better when I say I went to the Jim

*   *   *   *

My computer beat me in chess,
but I beat it in kickboxing

*   *   *   *

If people could read my mind,
I'd get punched in the face a lot

*   *   *   *

Pilates? I thought you said pie and lattes

*   *   *   *

I entered ten puns in a contest to see which would
win. No pun in ten did

*   *   *   *

My friend has a trophy wife
It obviously wasn't first place

*   *   *   *

I was watching commercials,
and a Thursday Night Football game broke out

*   *   *   *

For the game Sunday I'll bring chips
just in queso you need it

*   *   *   *

Doing this show is like being a tailpipe;
it's exhausting

*   *   *   *

I used to have a handle on life, but it broke

*   *   *   *

I'm using performance-enhancing chalk today

*   *   *   *

I'm been old school every since
I had to repeat first grade twice

*   *   *   *

Once you lick the icing off a cupcake,
it's just a boring muffin

*   *   *   *

I played water polo until my horse drowned

*   *   *   *

I party every night like a rock star, a poor rock star
without an instrument or a band or a place to play

*   *   *   *

I wish I had a dollar for every dollar I've wasted

*   *   *   *

Most days I lose on purpose
just to make the others feel better

*   *   *   *

I have a strange feeling I'm being watched now

*   *   *   *

If I have to start using facts here,
you're going to be in real trouble

*   *   *   *

I play microwave golf, 18 holes in three minutes

*   *   *   *

My chalkboard has never been hacked

*   *   *   *

Don't leave yet;
I may need somebody to blame for all this

*   *   *   *

Never trust atoms; they make up everything

*   *   *   *

My wallet is like an onion—when
I open it I start to cry

*   *   *   *

Birds of a feather always flock together—
to poop on my car

*   *   *   *

I had the smartest teacher in the world
I was self-taught

*   *   *   *

Could that be true?
My birth certificate just expired

*   *   *   *

Before there was Twitter, there was Twalkboard

*   *   *   *

Just be brief, no matter how long it takes

*   *   *   *

Unicorns are just skinny rhinos

*   *   *   *

I'm going to stop putting things off until
tomorrow, starting tomorrow

*   *   *   *

The chalkboard is gluten-free

*   *   *   *

Bad spellers of the world untie!

*   *   *   *

If speech is free, then why do they have to pay
for vowels on *Wheel Of Fortune?*

*   *   *   *

I thought I made a mistake, but I was mistaken

*   *   *   *

If I win Powerball, I will split it with all the
viewers if they can find me
on an island in the South Pacific

*   *   *   *

I would tell a joke about pizza,
but that would be too cheesy

*   *   *   *

I'm a contestant on a Reali-ty show

*   *   *   *

A door open is ajar
When a jar is open is it adoor?

*   *   *   *

That chandelier I passed before
was the high light of my day

*   *   *   *

I've fallen in love with the Internet
It was love at first site

*   *   *   *

Before you came along we were hungry
Now we are fed up!

*   *   *   *

Now go away, or I shall taunt you a second time

*   *   *   *

Moonlight becomes you,
total darkness even more!

*   *   *   *

People live and learn. He just lives

*   *   *   *

I'm dark and handsome
When it's dark, I'm handsome

*   *   *   *

I worship the ground that awaits you

*   *   *   *

Your argument is like the waves of the sea
It makes me sick!

* * * *

Your mouth is getting too big for your muzzle

* * * *

I discovered the python had a crush on me

* * * *

Sit down and give your mind a rest

* * * *

If brains were dynamite,
you couldn't blow your nose

* * * *

I'm not the most interesting man in the world, but
I beat him at Rock, Paper, Scissors,
and he had to buy the beer

* * * *

20

Every time I go into a locker room or on a practice field, pro and college athletes tell me how much they like the show, and the chalkboard sayings.

I lived on the Upper West Side of Manhattan for 2 ½ years and I would run into everybody from Engleberg Humperdinck to Al Pacino, and all of them would say how much they loved the chalkboard quotes. I walked out of an elevator in my apartment, and Bill Murray was getting on. I was stunned. He was laughing. "Love the blackboard," he said, and the door closed.

When I was waiting on that elevator another time, a man next to me said, "You're the sports guy with the blackboard, right?" I nodded. He introduced himself and said he owned one of Manhattan's most famous restaurants and a jazz club where famed guitarist Les Paul played.

"Talk for me." he said.

"Uh, why?"

"I see the show while I'm in the gym every day, and the sound's turned off, and the only thing I pay attention to is the chalkboard. I always wondered what you sound like."

I spoke.

"I think I still like the sayings on the chalkboard better," he said.

And that's OK.

If you have some sayings, send them to me at woody@woodypaige.com, and we'll do an updated version of this book. If you don't, we won't.

These are for those of you who asked for it.

*   *   *   *

Talk is cheap; chalk is $2.49 a box

*   *   *   *

Be yourself. Everyone else is already taken

*   *   *   *

Don't play stupid with me … I'm better at it

*   *   *   *

The next time you think you're perfect,
try walking on water

*   *   *   *

Raisin cookies? What a dumb idea!

*   *   *   *

I totally take back ... I can't remember

*   *   *   *

Winning ATH is like being
the champion of nothing

*   *   *   *

If each day is a gift,
I would like to know where I can return Mondays

*   *   *   *

Time is precious ... waste it wisely!

*   *   *   *

Relax, I'm harmless

*   *   *   *

Dear Algebra, stop asking me to find your X
Don't ask me Y

*   *   *   *

No one ignores me quite the way Tony
and my mom do

*   *   *   *

Normal is boring

*   *   *   *

Bad decisions make good stories

*   *   *   *

I mustache you a question

*   *   *   *

You couldn't handle me
even if I came with instructions

*   *   *   *

I should come with a warning label

*   *   *   *

I'm not arguing;
I'm just talking well above a whisper

*   *   *   *

I'm not stubborn. My way is just better

*   *   *   *

Don't hate what you can't imitate

*   *   *   *

You read my board
That's enough social interaction for today

*   *   *   *

For a minute there, you almost bored me to death

*   *   *   *

I'm non-flammable

*   *   *   *

I'm not childish, you're just a big doody head

*   *   *   *

I was much happier being in denial

*   *   *   *

Fake karate is better than no karate at all

*   *   *   *

I'm silently correcting your grammar

*   *   *   *

I've stopped listening;
why haven't you stopped talking?

*   *   *   *

I'm what Willis was talkin' 'bout

*   *   *   *

I changed my iPod's name to Titanic. It's syncing

*   *   *   *

This girl said she recognized me from the
vegetarian club, but I'd never met herbivore

*   *   *   *

I stayed up all night to see where the sun went.
Then it dawned on me

*   *   *   *

A guy with your IQ should have a low voice too!

*   *   *   *

Catastrophic success

*   *   *   *

I need a life
Do you know where I can download one?

*   *   *   *

Due to recent cutbacks,
the mute button has been turned off

*   *   *   *

Dear Tony, if I promise to miss you,
will you go away?

*   *   *   *

All 5 voices in my head agree:
"Cowlishaw is wrong"

*   *   *   *

Clockwood Orange

*   *   *   *

Down with words that actions speak louder than

*   *   *   *

A witty saying proves nothing

*   *   *   *

I'd humiliate you but I'm afraid you might like it

*   *   *   *

What are the cat days of summer?

*   *   *   *

I'm 14 in dog years

*   *   *   *

I'm here because I have to be:
what's your problem?

*   *   *   *

I have a master's degree in chalkboard sayings

*   *   *   *

Do you prefer cat-nip or cat-nap?

*   *   *   *

Cat didn't get my tongue ... mute did

*   *   *   *

My cat was hit by a car,
and now she's down to six lives

*   *   *   *

My dog attends disobedience school

*   *   *   *

Don't spend all your money on a safe

*   *   *   *

Hunger is the best sauce

*   *   *   *

My dad used to say the ice cream truck
plays music when it's out

*   *   *   *

What is it about "buy" or "sell"
that confuses the producers?

*   *   *   *

What is it about this question that confused
someone to leave out the question mark

*   *   *   *

I substitute fast reflexes for good manners

*   *   *   *

Boycott sham-poo! Demand real-poo!

*   *   *   *

Another brilliant mind ruined by this show

*   *   *   *

Ambition is a poor excuse for
not having enough sense to be lazy

*   *   *   *

When I'm not in my right mind,
my left mind gets pretty crowded

*   *   *   *

I'm not cheap, but I am on special this week

*   *   *   *

I can never tell when I run out of invisible chalk

*   *   *   *

I hope life isn't a joke, because I don't get it

*   *   *   *

I drive way too fast to worry about cholesterol

*   *   *   *

Whenever I find the key to success,
someone changes the lock

*   *   *   *

Two horses in a man costume

*   *   *   *

Make a mental note ... oh,
I see you're out of paper

*   *   *   *

Make somebody happy. Mind your own business!

*   *   *   *

Every golf shot makes somebody happy

*   *   *   *

Keep talking. I always yawn when I'm interested

*   *   *   *

He does the work of 3 men:
Moe, Larry, and Curly

*   *   *   *

I didn't wanna say "buy", but I couldn't say "sell"

*   *   *   *

I'm a victim of "soicumstance"

*   *   *   *

Don't think, it may sprain your brain!

*   *   *   *

If fools could fly, Around The Horn
would be an airport

*   *   *   *

If brains were rain, you'd be a desert

*   *   *   *

If I said anything to you that I should be sorry for,
I'm glad

*   *   *   *

If you stand close enough to him,
you can hear the ocean

*   *   *   *

He's so ugly he trick or treats over the phone

*   *   *   *

His suitcase doesn't have a handle

*   *   *   *

I hear the only place you're ever invited is outside

*   *   *   *

Someday you'll go far,
if you catch the right plane on time

*   *   *   *

The only thing Pablo brought to this show
was his car

*   *   *   *

I'm busy now. Can I ignore you some other time?

*   *   *   *

You're getting on my nerves,
and I only have two left!

*   *   *   *

I'd never forget the first time we met—although
I'll make an exception in this case

*   *   *   *

If you don't like my opinion of you—
improve yourself!

*   *   *   *

I understand you Bill, but I talk to walls

*   *   *   *

If I had a face like yours, I'd sue my parents!

*   *   *   *

Of all the hosts in the history of this show,
Tony is my 2nd favorite of both

*   *   *   *

People say I've no taste, but I like you

*   *   *   *

He's so dense that light bends around him

*   *   *   *

Your brother was an only child

*   *   *   *

Tim Cowlishaw has the IQ of lint

*   *   *   *

For Lent, I'm giving up lint

*   *   *   *

Brains aren't everything. In fact,
in your case they're nothing!

*   *   *   *

He has more faces than Mount Rushmore

*   *   *   *

In the land of the witless, I'm the king

*   *   *   *

Izzy isn't is he?

*   *   *   *

Converse with any plankton lately?

*   *   *   *

Krusty, Clarabell, Bozo, Doink and
Woody applying for ref jobs

*   *   *   *

Tony, I found an endorsement deal for you:
"Just for Dorks" hair coloring

*   *   *   *

I'm going to memorize your name and
throw my head away

*   *   *   *

Plaschke can think without moving his lips!

*   *   *   *

Don't you love nature, despite what it did to you?

*   *   *   *

Don't feel bad. A lot of people have no talent

*   *   *   *

As an outsider, what do you think
of the human race?

*   *   *   *

They say it's mind over matter
I say it doesn't matter

*   *   *   *

You're very smart
You have brains you've never used

*   *   *   *

I bought a really cool shovel
It was groundbreaking

*   *   *   *

If you're not shore, don't give into pier pressure

*   *   *   *

In golf, you should wear 2 pairs of pants
in case you get a hole in one

*   *   *   *

If I could talk I would tell you
to stop writing on me!

*   *   *   *

Chalkboreds don't have spell check

*   *   *   *

If I could be in 2 places at once,
I'd love to meet myself

*   *   *   *

Thank me. I'm welcome

*   *   *   *

What's the iPhone's favorite football team
the Chargers?

*   *   *   *

I stole the iPhone 5, but I never faced time

*   *   *   *

For me, failure always must be my first option

*   *   *   *

Maybe we should mute Tony
so he can get his beauty rest

*   *   *   *

For my next trick, Bomani will be eliminated

*   *   *   *

You have to learn to finish your sentences because

*   *   *   *

Got chalk!

*   *   *   *

21

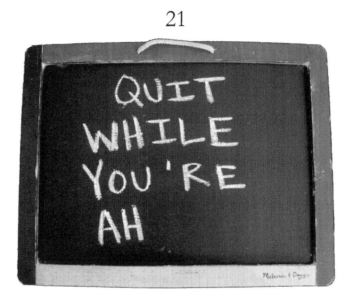

Acknowledgements

*   *   *   *

I'm Almost Out of Cha: Woody Paige's Chalkboard Tales was written and produced with the guidance, assistance and support of, literally, a multitude of people.

The blackboard and I thank you all.

The thanks begin with the viewers. They have kept the program (and me AND the chalkboard) on the air for 11 years with their loyalty.

I've heard from tens of thousands of viewers by email, phone and snail mail, Facebook, Twitter and now, Tout, or in person in airports, at arenas and in stadiums, in bars, restaurants, locker rooms and on the street. Recently in Indianapolis I left my wallet at the Frontier Airlines counter for a brief time. The customer representative paged me in the airport and made an announcement about my wallet, which was rather embarrassing. Dozens of passengers, TSA reps (who gave me a U.S. Department of Transportation document, a get out of jail card, to get past security in case I didn't have my identifications) and airport workers approached to tell me I had forgotten my wallet—and to mention how much they enjoy the chalkboard sayings. Amazing.

Over the years viewers have submitted hundreds of sayings they've made up or heard at work or in a war, spotted on bumper stickers or a T-shirt or in a book, and, as one said, "This quote has been passed down in my family for generations." Some we couldn't use on the air or in mixed company. Others we couldn't use because they made no sense.

Thanks to all of you, especially the contributors who share in this book.

It's been stunning how many people ask, "When are you going to compile the chalkboard sayings in a book?" For years, I sort of dismissed the proposal, wondering who would care enough to buy the book, but with the help of Jason Weindruch, my 11-year associate on the show (and the man who has such fine penmanship and chalks the chalk), and Heather Domko, who filled in regularly for Jason over a seven-year span (and now works on *House Hunters* and other cable programs and network commercials), we were able to find every chalkboard saying used on the show. Heather actually flew from Denver to the headquarters of the show in Washington, D.C., a few years ago and went through the tapes of all the shows (at fast forward, of course) and wrote down every quote. For the past several years Jason kept track of every chalkboard quote, and he's been assisted in the project lately by our new production assistant David Briggs.

Jason also bought the first miniature blackboard at a "Toys R' Us" in New York about 9 years ago and then found perfectly-sized chalkboards from Melissa & Doug, a husband-and-wife company started in a garage 25 years ago. Doug and Melissa and their employees hand-make the blackboards and other educational toys, and we've purchased dozens (at $19.99). We donate the used blackboards to charities for auctions or give them to special individuals— children in hospitals and adults who have served in the military and been wounded.

Thanks, Jason, for being there for the birth of a crazy idea and its long life. Jason is off to New York City to become a big-time TV producer.

David Vigliano, the owner, CEO and head agent of Vigliano Associates, the preeminent boutique literary agency in New York City, believed in the book project and agreed to publish the E-reader book and, potentially, a hardback or a paperback and, even, a year desk calendar of the blackboard sayings. David has represented 16 No. 1 New York Times best-sellers, and 60 books that have reached the Times list since 2002. He also recently published *Drunk On Sports*, an inspiring book by another original *Around The Horn* co-panelist, Tim Cowlishaw. Read Tim's book next.

I met months ago at a Manhattan restaurant with David and editor Thomas Flannery, Jr. who took on the responsibilities of overseeing the book throughout the process. He came up with the title and had the idea of utilizing photos of the actual blackboard quotes to begin each chapter. Thomas did the proofreading and made the suggestion of including tales about some of the sayings. Thank you, David, for persevering and leading me through a forest where I couldn't see the trees.

Any mistakes in this book are mine.

Without David and Thomas, there would be no book. Thanks, guys, for believing.

My business partner Eric "Tre" Rudig, who owns Youdigrudig Media LLC, took all the photos of the blackboard sayings. In the past year and a half Tre has provided me with a wealth of information and help in social media and produced and managed my website.

My close friends Tony and Paul Carter allowed me to stay at their fantastic home in Marathon, Fla., on several occasions to write (and rewrite) chapters in the book while I sat and stared at the Gulf of Mexico, and the sunsets, just off their deck and dock. Then, at night, Tony and I retired to Porky's to eat barbecue, watch sports and drink a beer, or three.

Thanks also to friends Dennis Whitelaw and J.D. "Yogi" Kirst for having to put up with my drivel while I wrote.

Mark Shapiro and Jim Cohen first asked me to contribute to a series of documentaries, SportsCentury, in the late 1990s. My role was to sit in a hotel conference room (set up to appear as an English manor library) and the producer would bark out a famous sports name, and I would respond with a sports story or an opinion. During the course of a day I would comment on 100 athletes, coaches and a horse (Secretariat). There were no rehearsals, I had no clue what the responses would be used for.

At the turn of the millennium, my lady friend and I were on a cruise ship in the Panama Canal (it seemed to be a good place, given all the dire predictions about the end of the world as we knew it), and preparing to celebrate New Year's Eve, and the beginning of 2000, when she said, "You're on TV." "I can't be on TV. I'm in the Panama Canal." But there I was talking about Michael Jordan. He had just been named the No. 1 Athlete of the Century. I told a story about Jordan being sick during the Finals in Salt Lake City, and the two of us talking outside the arena before the game, and he throwing up as I sat on a picnic table.

Shapiro and Cohen made my TV career. Thanks.

Thanks Bill Rasmussen, George Bodenheimer, John Skipper, and Norby Williamson for creating and shaping the network and my very minor role in it.

I became close friends with Max Kellerman & Bill Wolff, two men who have gone to greater things in broadcasting. And they would introduce me to young Michael Price, who would become my agent and one of my closest friends. Michael has represented me for the past 10 years, even if he didn't have to. He has one of the best agencies in Beverly Hills and represents some of the top names in television and movies, and produces outstanding sports cable shows, and I'm at the bottom of his food chain. But Michael always has treated me as if I'm his only client. He is who Jerry McGuire really wanted to be. Thanks, Michael, for your counsel since this book was a germ; and I mean germ. He also represents Tony Reali and helped persuade Tony to write the foreword. The young Reali, who looked 12 but actually was 26, made the show more about interaction among the panelists, and excelled with his wit, his writing and creative intelligence. Reali is a genuine rising star. Erik Rydholm is a calming force and a genius. When times have been tough for me, Erik always has been there. Aaron Solomon runs the day-to-day operation with class and composure. He tells me most often, "Shut up, you're killing me." I like Aaron. Thanks, Aaron, for being on my side … occasionally.

If I had a brother, I would want him to be John Dursee. He deserves thanks and a piece of the action. Remember the name Josh Bard. He is the most imaginative young man I've worked with. Myriam Leger is "The Voice" you hear on the show introducing the sponsors. She is the sharpest, nicest person, and always asks about my mother. And Mark Hancock is the best researcher in the game. If Mitt Romney had been elected President,

Mark, who took time off to work for his campaign, would have become the first U.S. Secretary of Stats.

I also want to thank all the other members of the crew: Bonnie Berko, Tracey Roberts, Clarence Williams, Wiliam "Mars" Lewis, Alex Staherski, Brian Haas, Robert Mitton, Tony Graves, Sean Finn, Greg Hopper, Jeff McDonald, James Mirsky, Sean Creech, Kevin, Ceigersmidt, Cathy "The First" Noel, Bobby Ferarra, Chris Gavin, Tim Farrell, Delano Bell, Deborah Pepper, Kelia Williams, Bill Kramer, Richard Southcott and Buck Parr. I'm not much, but without them, I'm nothing.

As I've stated, chalkboard sayings have come from the unfertile minds of me and Jason, viewers, friends, relatives, wait staff, websites and trash cans. Others were inspired or expressed in some way by the writings of Benjamin Franklin, Dorothy Parker, Kurt Vonnegut, Oscar Wilde, Winston Churchill, W. C. Fields, actors, dancers and William Shakespeare. Books, compilations and authors that also have been thought-provoking, good reads and contributors include: *Anguished English*, by Richard Lederer, *The Dictionary Of Cliches* by James Rogers, *Quotations With An Attitude* by Roy L. Stewart, *2,715 One-Line Quotations for Speakers, Writers and Raconteurs* by Edward F. Murphy, *The Bumper Stick Book* by Michael & Dawn Reilly, *Great One Liners* edited by Marcia Kamien, *Zingers, Quips and One-Liners* edited by Geoff Tibballs and *Hilarious Roasts, Toasts and One-Liners* by Gene Perrett with Terry Martin.

Thanks to the other panelists, especially the originals: Cowlishaw, Bob Ryan, Jackie McMullen, Jay Mariotti, Kevin Blackistone ,T.J. Simers, my friend and solid rock Bill Plaschke, J.A. Adande, Michael Smith, Michael Holley, Gene Wojciechowski, Charlie Pierce, Bomani Jones, Jemele Hill, Israel Gutierrez, Pablo S. Torre, Jim Armstrong and Mark Kiszla and Adam Schefter in Denver,

Josh Elliott, Andy Katz, Bruce Arthur, Ron Borges, Mark Cuban, Bob Glauber, Frank Isola, Richard Justice, John Powers, Dan Shanoff, Jean-Jacques Taylor and Lil Wayne.

My daughter Shannon has never paid attention to the show, especially the chalkboard sayings. Maybe she finally will read them. Probably not.

My sincerest thanks and love for Jerry, who was there for and with me.

I appreciate that Laurie Orlando and David Brofsky have been particularly encouraging, and professional, to me for many years.

Finally, without Woodrow Wilson Paige Sr. and Billie Montgomery Paige, I wouldn't be on TV or even around. My mom, the classic and classy Southern lady, is my biggest fan and never misses a show, except on Thursdays when Dr. Phil has special topics. On my most recent birthday I asked her to describe our first house when I was born. "Your father and I moved in with my mother in a three-room house. She had the bedroom; Woodrow and I lived in the front room." And where was I sleeping? She replied, "In a drawer in the kitchen."

In 1947 my parents bought a house with a $20 monthly mortgage, "And that was the hardest times we ever had. Your dad made a dollar a day." Daddy's mom died when he was 2; his father abandoned him. Woody Sr. slept on front porches of Mississippi farms and picked cotton. At 7, he became very ill, nearly died and spent a year in a charity hospital ward, where he was diagnosed with juvenile diabetes and taught himself to read from Life Magazine. The recent discovery of insulin kept him alive.

He tried to join the U.S. Navy at the outbreak of World War II. He lied about his age and his illness and was being sworn in when my aunt ran in screaming. He got a job on a Mississippi River barge until the captain found his insulin needles, and he was fired. He found work sweeping floors. He educated himself, met my mother, and they had me when they were dirt-poor teenagers. He took me to my first college football game (Tennessee vs. Ole Miss) when I was 18 months old. It snowed the entire game. Maybe he was trying to tell me something. He bought me a football when I was 7, a typewriter when I was 8. He would become a successful department store chain executive, traveled on a plane for the first time to New York on a buying trip and brought me three souvenirs; miniatures of the Empire State Building and the Statue of Liberty and a stack of newspapers sports sections and said, "Someday you'll go to New York and become a big star as a sports writer." We couldn't dream about TV. We didn't own one. Fifty years later, when I joined ESPN full time in New York, I was shown to my new office on the seventh floor in the New Yorker Hotel at 8th and Broadway. Directly out the window was the Empire State Building. I closed the door and cried. "Dad," I said to myself, "I finally made it." He didn't. My daddy never saw me on *Around The Horn*. Woodrow Sr. died from life-long diabetic complications at 49.

His most famous saying to me was, "Son, if that's a monkey wrench you just handed me, I will drive you downtown to Court Square tomorrow, give you an hour to draw a crowd, and I will kiss your butt at high noon in front of God and everybody."

Thank you, sir, for showing me how to recognize and use a monkey wrench, introducing me to sports and writing, teaching me how to be witty and charming, hard-working and humble, and helping me to realize not to take myself and a chalkboard seriously.

Made in the USA
Lexington, KY
15 May 2014